ENCHANTMENT

Wonder in modern life

Praise for *Enchantment: Wonder in Modern Life*

'Understanding begins – and ends – in wonder. This book articulates simply, and in a personal and unpretentious manner, an urgently needed defence of wonder as indispensable to a true perception and just appreciation of the world. We neglect its message at our peril.'

Iain McGilchrist, author of *The Master and his Emissary*

'An impressive erudition and literary sensibility animate the pages of this thoughtful book. With a light poetic touch Curry traces the many ways in which enchantment lies at the core of human experience, even in a world that does its best to disabuse and disillusion us. Detaching it from ideology, Curry sees enchantment as an irrepressible mode of our being present to things, and vice versa. The enchanted moments cannot be sustained yet they lay their claim on us time and time again by virtue of the fact that we are alive and capable of wonder.'

Robert Pogue Harrison, author of *Forests: The Shadow of Civilization*

'What could be more confounding than trying to understand 'enchantment', an uncanny power that by its very nature frustrates all comprehension? Yet in this small volume Patrick Curry accomplishes much. If we join him as he tracks several of the numberless styles of enchantment, if we pay heed to his insights and sometimes argue with him, we'll find ourselves slowly becoming more layered within ourselves, wiser, and maybe even wonder-struck.'

David Abram, author of *The Spell of the Sensuous* and *Becoming Animal*

ENCHANTMENT

Wonder in
modern life

PATRICK CURRY

Floris
Books

The world is its own magic.

Shunryu Suzuki

First published in 2019 by Floris Books
First published in North America in 2020
© 2019 Patrick Curry

R.S. Thomas is quoted from his *Collected Poems* (London: Phoenix, 1993),
with kind permission from The Orion Publishing Group.

Ono no Komachi is quoted from *The Ink Dark Moon: Love Poems by Ono
no Komachi and Izumi Shikibu*, trans. Jane Hirschfield with Mariko Aratani
(New York: Vintage Books, 1990), with kind permission from Penguin
Random House LLC.

 Also available as an eBook

Typesetting by User Design, Illustration
and Typesetting, UK
British Library CIP Data available
ISBN 978-178250-609-6
Printed in Great Britain by Bell & Bain Ltd

 Floris Books supports sustainable forest management by
printing this book on materials made from wood that comes
from responsible sources and reclaimed material

MIX
Paper from
responsible sources
FSC® C007785

Contents

1. Introduction

What is enchantment? Its moments are short but deep: eyes meet, and everything has changed – sharing a perfect meal, both the food and the love with which it was cooked, with a few close friends – walking through a landscape charged with mystery – being carried away by glorious music... Most simply, enchantment is an experience of wonder. Variations include awe, amazement, astonishment. It can vary in intensity from charm, through delight, to full-blown joy. Most of what I have to say concerns the last, or what we could call 'radical enchantment'. As we shall see, such experiences are fundamental to being alive.

Any attempt to understand and appreciate enchantment requires respecting its integrity. That includes resisting the urge to explain it away or reduce it to something else, whether 'up' to God or 'down' to neurophysiology. It may be impossible to define precisely – indeed, being indefinable is essential to any acceptable definition of it – but that doesn't mean it doesn't matter. Many important things are like that.

Almost anything can enchant, from orchids, fonts, motorcycles, incense and cheese to perfumes, comics and kites (both the kind that flies and the kind you fly). Enchantment is nonetheless a particular phenomenon, because we are a particular kind of being – the human kind. Despite our many differences, we share some fundamental traits, needs and abilities. As a result, some contexts for enchantment are more common than others. After we explore its principal dynamics, therefore, we shall turn to how they play out in love, in art, in religion, in food, in learning and in nature.

Enchantment also has certain recurring characteristics. They are not easy to describe, because one of them is that it only happens in, and in response to, precise actual circumstances. It cannot be separated, in practice, from its contexts. Here are a few first-hand reports in which some of those characteristics – notably a slightly weird combination of sensuality and spirituality – are already evident.

A textile maker and collector: 'I have spent countless hours collecting old *Tsutsugaki*, indigo blue cotton cloth with the patterns done with a *tsutsubiki* tube-drawn technique. I was captivated by their dynamic beauty and could not resist their charm. Each one was new, different and irresistible'. A perfumer on Chanel No. 5 by Ernest Beaux (1921): it 'gives the irresistible impression of a smooth, continuously curved, gold-coloured volume that stretches deliciously, like a sleepy panther, from top note to drydown.' And a motorcycle enthusiast on her 'bike of the mind' (which is very like her white Moto Guzzi Lario): 'I fear it; often I dream about it; sometimes I love it with longing as if it were already gone'.

Why does enchantment matter? Its moments don't cancel out suffering. They can exist alongside it, however, and even provide solace. What the philosopher Max Weber summarised as 'undeserved suffering, unpunished injustice, and hopeless stupidity' remains as comprehensive a catalogue as ever, and we cannot blame anyone whose life has blotted out enchantment. But to deny it on principle would simply add to the misery. Why shouldn't anyone welcome it into their lives when they can? Sometimes enchantment makes life worth living. It can even be life-changing. Far from being a matter of psychology, a purely subjective state of mind, enchantment can reveal profound truths, lead to deep values, and become central to a life well-lived. So, in closing, we shall turn to how to live in a way that is open to enchantment, and even works with it.

Before then, however, we shall consider the contraries of enchantment: not only its simple absence but disenchantment, and what I call 'glamour'. That brings us to Weber's famous prediction, almost a prophecy, uttered one hundred years ago, of 'the disenchantment of the world'. Weber was at least right about this: there are indeed powerful enemies of enchantment, with a programme to disenchant the world. That doesn't mean they have things all their own way, however. So we shall look at to what extent, and in what ways, the world is now disenchanted.

It is important that we don't succumb to seeing enchantment everywhere and in everything, that it is as definite as may be for something that is essentially non-verbal (even when words spark it off). To that end, contrasting enchantment with what it is not is instructive. Most obviously, when you are disenchanted – and, inseparably, when the world is disenchanted – it is an experience of abstract time and space. Both exist only as bits, one temporal and the other spatial but all in identical units, so it can truly be said that when you've seen one you've seen 'em all. Hence its boredom and ultimately nihilism.

Enchantment couldn't be more different. It consists of a unique moment and a unique place, and it is saturated with meaning. From the (disenchanted) outside it appears tiny and limited, but it is actually bigger on the (enchanted) inside. In fact, as a character in John Crowley's novel *Little, Big* says, 'The farther in you go, the bigger it gets,' before adding, 'until, at the center point, it is infinite. Or at least very, very large.' By the same token, time stops. Or at least, goes very, very slowly. (I mean time as we live it, not as measured by a clock.)

However, the difference between infinite and very large, or stopping and slowing, is important, because an enchanted place is not quite infinite, and the moment, however endless while it's happening, will not last forever. Eventually the gently revolving eddy, temporarily sheltered by some fortuitous rocks near the bank, will find its way back into the rushing stream. As a consequence, the end of enchantment is already implicit in its occurrence. Every 'hello' of wonder is shadowed by a 'goodbye'; hence its poignancy.

Enchantment also differs from two other ways of being. To characterise these I have borrowed from classical Greek myth. One we can call Apollonian. This is the mode of coldly rational mastery, achieved through imposing order and system. Others are treated as objects to be dominated, manipulated or exploited, and the other's value is instrumental; it is valuable only for how it may be used for some purpose or other. Enchantment, in contrast, is nothing if not a relationship between two subjects (the other subject can be almost anyone or anything) and for the enchanted person, the other's value is intrinsic. It needs, and can find, no further justification; we have reached bedrock.

The second mode is Dionysian: pleasure, rising to ecstasy and potentially culminating in union whereby the experiencing subject, being extinguished, vanishes. It is hot, emotional and overwhelming. Again, in contrast, even radical enchantment doesn't obliterate boundaries. It simply crosses them, rendering them permeable. In this process, as the psychologist Ethel Spector Person says, 'paradoxically the self is neither lost nor diminished. Quite the contrary, the self is affirmed and enriched.' Indeed, if there were no boundaries at all enchantment would become impossible, because there would be no subjects to meet and experience each other. One may experience enchantment as oneness, but as W.H. Auden says, 'for there to be one, first there must be two.' And although light and delicate compared to Dionysian passion, enchantment can be piercing.

We shall be mainly concerned with enchantment in individual lives. There are collective enchantments, however. Examples include the spontaneous reactions to the fall of the Berlin Wall in 1989, the death of Princess Diana in 1997, and the Charlie Hebdo murders in Paris in 2015. In all three there was a powerful emotional response, cutting across class, gender and race, which was completely spontaneous. This was accompanied by a common perception of what these events actually meant, their significance, that was equally uninfluenced by elite opinion. In fact, these responses left many in government, the media and the professional intelligentsia stranded between scrambling to get on message, fearful of being left behind, and contemptuous dismissal of the irrational masses. (Ironically, such hostility is itself often more visceral than reasoned.)

Thinking, which is as natural to humans as feeling or willing, is not a problem for enchantment. Rational*ism*, or any other 'ism', for that matter, is. An explanation for everything, even if only in principle, reduces everything to some greater cause. That makes rationalism inherently disenchanting. We need not engage in it, however, and can choose otherwise. Theory, *theōria* in Greek, originally referred to going elsewhere on a pilgrimage, participating in their religious ritual, and reporting what happened upon returning home. To retrieve the wisdom long buried in modern meanings of the word 'philosophy', we must, as Wittgenstein says, 'do away with all *explanation*, and description alone must take its place'.

The modern academy, unfortunately, loves explanation more than wisdom, and method much more than direct encounter. Its few studies of enchantment therefore mostly reduce it sideways, so to speak, to something else: the sublime, the uncanny, the sacred and so on. But you won't find out much if your starting-point is that the phenomenon in question is really something else we already understand (or think we do). What follows here, instead, is what I have found out from *not* knowing, guided only by own experiences, thinking and knowledge garnered along the way. Sometimes I have been inspired and guided by a few earlier explorers; but there too, I have had to trust my own instincts. What's the alternative?

A personal note seems appropriate, then, since I make no pretence of an impossibly 'objective' survey. My purpose in writing this book was to better understand and appreciate enchantment and perhaps, in sharing it, to help others do so too. That desire grew out of an abiding love of wonder, sometimes sober, sometimes passionate, in ways that I am only noticing now. But I have been equally shaped by a fear, sometimes bordering on terror, of its lack – sheer meaninglessness – as well as a hatred of disenchantment, its opposite. (The lack and the opposite of enchantment, as we shall see, are not the same thing.) Why? I don't know, and although it's fun to speculate I don't think it's finally all that important. What matters is to work with what you're given, and give something back.

2. The Dynamics of Enchantment

Perhaps more than anything else, enchantment is a matter of relationship. That in turn requires each party to be distinctive and therefore different, creating a gap between them over which they can meet. That is turn creates a 'third thing', something new in the world: a metaphorical you-*and*-me, or a this-but-*also*-that. We shall explore this dynamic further in a moment, but for now it's important to notice that without gaps, boundaries and differences to cross – provided they are not too great to bridge at all – no meeting can take place. Dionysian total unity and Apollonian hyper-separation are equally hostile to enchantment.

[handwritten marginal note: Martin Buber]

Not all or any relationships will do, however. Auden makes a vital distinction between true and false enchantment. True enchantment seeks only the continued existence and well-being of the beloved other person, place, artefact or whatever. In the words of J.R.R. Tolkien, another reliable guide to enchantment (and Auden's tutor), it is 'a love and respect for all things, "animate" and "inanimate", an unpossessive love of them as "other"'. False enchantment, on the other hand, desires either to possess the other – which aligns it with the Apollonian mode of mastery-over – or to be possessed by it, as with the Dionysian mode of ecstatic absorption in a greater whole.

The heart of true enchantment is sheer existential wonder, so any pathology results from what we have brought to it. If there is a worm at its heart, we put it there. Whether we can altogether avoid doing so is another matter. Unchecked, the desire to possess or be possessed can tip us into addiction and destruction. But there is no stain on enchantment itself. Even its passing only becomes a problem with our attachment to it staying, although nothing could be more understandable. Sometimes we simply cannot give it up. Then it can happen as it did to Karen Blixen, when she had to leave her beloved East Africa. She found she couldn't; rather, 'it was the country slowly and gravely withdrawing from me'.

The relatively selfless love of true enchantment also contrasts with passive narcissism, egotism and self-importance, and with active cruelty. The stronger the enchantment, the more one is in a real relationship with the other. Rather than dominating or manipulating the other as an object, or being treated oneself as an object, one is sensed as well as sensing, apprehended by as much as apprehending.

As this view implies, whatever enchants becomes, in effect, another person. Whether the other party is technically a human or not, or even alive or not, is unimportant. This is not a matter of 'projecting', 'anthropomorphising', or any of the other modern strategies of disenchantment whereby human privilege is preserved. (As if only we were sentient!) No one who has experienced the wonder of connecting, at a deep level, with another being of any kind should allow themselves to be bullied out of it by intellectual authorities. As Wittgenstein says, 'if all things behave as though a sign had meaning, then it does'.

Borrowing from myth and fairy tale, Tolkien's own term for enchantment was *Faërie* – a place which contains, he said, not only fairies, dwarves, trolls or dragons but more importantly ourselves, when we are enchanted, together with whatever we are enchanted by. Potentially, therefore, it holds the Sun, Moon and Earth and all things that are in it. *Faërie* is where we find ourselves when we are enchanted, and it becomes wherever we are at that moment.

There is a catch, however. Because we are human beings, we cannot actually live there. If we are lucky we may visit it, or it may visit us, and perhaps return, but we cannot stay. As in fairy-stories, sooner or later we find ourselves on the disenchanted outside again, our pockets full of dry leaves that a moment before had been gold coins. The currency of enchantment has as little purchase in the 'real' world – so-called by those who either know no better or are bitter about their expulsion – as the reverse.

The experience of enchantment, no matter how delicious, is therefore often shot through with a poignant intimation of its end. Every presence is attended by an absence, which can then become a strange sort of presence. In Japanese culture, this realisation is termed *mono no aware*. The bittersweet quality of such enchantment is encapsulated, for example, in a haiku by the poet Bashō: 'Even in Kyōto, hearing the cuckoo cry, I long for Kyōto'. Auden says that at such times there are two temptations to be avoided: to deny the enchantment ever happened or was real, and to attempt to recover it by sheer will, perhaps through alcohol or other drugs. Simple appreciation that one *was* so blessed might help.

I think we are aware of this existential fact, even if often in denial. The novelist Elizabeth Bowen, leaving the city she loved and had been living in, put it off until the last possible moment: 'Only from the train as it moved did I look at Rome. Backs of houses I had not ever seen before wavered into mists, stinging my eyes. My darling, my darling, my darling. Here we have no abiding city.'

In order to have a healthy relationship with enchantment, what is needed is therefore not a weak or muddled or suggestible ego but precisely a strong one, with relatively secure boundaries, enabling one to resist the impulse to clutch at enchantment or vainly try to recapture it. For enchantment is wild and unbiddable. This fact follows from the essential dynamic of true relationship: no one is in control and outcomes are unpredictable, because its centre, being between two or more parties, cannot simply be occupied by any one of them. No one is in charge. That is why enchantment can occur at all. So it can be invited but never commanded, and when it comes, as the philosopher William James says, it comes 'in the manner of a gift or not at all'. For that reason, it is also neither necessarily fair nor just. I'm afraid *Faërie* is not a meritocracy. Like intelligence, talent and beauty, it isn't a reward for the deserving.

It follows that if enchantment is apparently being ordered, manipulated or created at will, it has been disappeared (thanks to the Argentinian military, this is now also a transitive verb) and replaced by something else. I call this simulacrum 'glamour'. The advertising industry above all (including Google and Facebook) doesn't want you to know the difference. Artists do. You can arrange the conditions for enchantment perfectly – the best this, that and the other – but it may or may not attend the opening. The same is true in our lives.

This means there is no method for achieving enchantment, nor re-enchantment. Not in the sense that people want and expect of a method, which they think of as scientific but is actually magical: if you do this, then that will happen. As soon as you are thinking about how to do something to bring about a desired outcome, you have already sacrificed the indispensable requirement: a direct encounter with another presence. You are already not paying attention, because you're doing something else. As Eugen Rosenstock-Huessy says, 'We always come to each other and even to ourselves too late as soon as we wish to know in advance what to do.' So there can be no *Ten Steps to an Enchanted Life/World* that is not a con. (*Some Things You Can Do that Might Help Keep Enchantment Alive in Your Life?* Okay.)

To borrow a term from the writer and explorer Freya Stark, the best attitude towards enchantment is fearless receptivity: neither a desire to extend one's self nor to lose one's self – which are equally issues of power – but simply having the intention to pay attention, here and now, to come what may. This isn't as easy as it might sound. It requires practice in what another poet, John Keats, famously called 'negative capability', that is, being 'capable of being in uncertainties, mysteries, doubts, without any irritable reaching after fact and reason'.

Certain conditions appear to be conducive to enchantment, among which fearless receptivity is the most important. Given its wildness, however, nothing can be said to *cause* it. To believe otherwise is to entertain the illusion that you can control it, which is mistaken and therefore damaging. Try to do so and you will end up with mere glamour.

The relationship between enchantment and power is complex. On the one hand, they are immiscible, like oil and water; where one predominates, the other is absent. On the other hand, artists of all kinds (as well as practitioners of religious ritual) must use all the will and skill they can muster to arrange those conducive conditions. But that arranging must be done knowing and respecting that the final say is not ours. So wonder and will are sometimes entangled, but they remain distinct. By the same token, enchantment can always happen spontaneously and unexpectedly.

There is a powerful resonance between enchantment as wild and nature as wild. As David Abram says, nature thoroughly includes humankind and our cultural creations, yet it also vastly exceeds humankind. Hence his term for nature: "the more-than-human world". Nature is therefore not under our control. If it appears to be, then it too has been replaced by something else we do think we own and can manage: some version of Nature Inc. arranged to suit human convenience. Positively, the ultimate source of enchantment, no matter how sophisticated, refined or complex, is nature. After all, we are entirely natural beings, even if it is part of our nature to be cultural, intellectual, religious, artistic, scientific and so on.

'Concrete Magic'

Enchantment is always an embodied encounter in an actual set of circumstances with a highly specific, indeed unique, other: *this* person or *this* place or *this* work, *here* and at *this* moment. It is therefore never abstract, generic or universal. Like the natural world, when it has not been wholly industrialised and instrumentalised for our purposes, enchantment is what Weber calls 'concrete magic'.

What he means is that enchantment is both embodied and embedded, in and of this world, *and* spiritual, ineffable and deeply mysterious. That 'magic' is not something added to the precise, concrete circumstances, or floating above it; it is immanent in and as them. As the poet Michael Longley observes, 'When you capture something with precision, you also release its mysterious aura. You don't get the mystery without the precision'. And what is the mystery that is released? It is the inexhaustible meaning of the precise other, their significance in a way that is, in effect, ultimate. In other words, enchantment, although thoroughly carnal, opens a door on the spiritual idea of that particular person, place or thing: what Blixen calls 'The idea God had when He made you'.

Another philosopher, Maurice Merleau-Ponty, describes what we are talking about as 'an idea that is not the contrary of the sensible', but rather is 'its lining and its depth'. And its aura is mysterious because we can never exhaust it, plumb its depths, explain it away. Unlike an abstraction like a formula, for example, an actual person or thing is inexhaustible in its specificity. This experience is transcendent, but it results from going deeper into things, not rising above them or leaving them behind. In its sheer presence, what Jan Zwicky (both poet and philosopher) describes as the enchanting other's 'radiant specificity' is not undermined or negated by vulnerability to time and chance. On the contrary, that is what makes it unique and precious, even as it is burning out, fading away or falling.

One of the best records of radical enchantment is that of Aldous Huxley, recalling what happened when he took mescaline the morning of 6 May 1953 in Los Angeles. (It is significant, by the way, that his primary motive was simply curiosity. He was not trying to make a certain predetermined state of mind happen, something that would have unavoidably turned into the false enchantment that drugs make all too easy.) What struck Huxley, as he beheld some flowers in a vase, was that:

> Plato seems to have made the enormous, the grotesque mistake of separating Being from becoming and identifying it with the mathematical abstraction of the Idea. He could never, poor fellow, have seen a bunch of flowers shining with their own inner light and all but quivering under the pressure of the significance with which they were charged; could never have perceived that what rose and iris and carnation so intensely signified was

nothing more, and nothing less, than what they were – a transience that was yet eternal life, a perpetual perishing that was at the same time pure Being...

As this account shows, enchantment's concrete magic ignores the supposedly radical difference between spiritual and physical, mental and material, and eternal and passing that has for so long bedevilled Western metaphysics. It continues to do so, thanks to that split's two institutionalised castes, usually representatives of religion and science respectively. While arguing over which pole is true and which illusory, however, they tacitly support each other. Both parties therefore misunderstand and mistrust enchantment; it calls their privileged position as representatives of the Truth into question. When Richard Dawkins and an Anglican bishop met in a radio broadcast, the one thing they could agree on was the iniquity of a common form of popular enchantment, astrology. But from their own points of view they're not entirely wrong, because the presence of enchantment is potentially subversive of modernity itself, of how the world was and is still being made modern. After all, wonder is literally price-less and use-less, both spiritually and materially, so those who value it nonetheless are indeed heretics.

Deep Moments

Something strange happens to time when you are in *Faërie*. Here are two accounts, one autobiographical and one fictional. The first is by Patrick Leigh Fermor, describing his experience of writing, years later, about a 'luminous moment' when, as a young man, he lingered long on a bridge between then-Czechoslovakia and Hungary.

I found it impossible to tear myself from my station and plunge into Hungary. I feel the same disability now: a momentary reluctance to lay hands on this particular fragment of the future: not out of fear but because, within arm's reach and still intact, this future seemed, and still seems, so full of promised marvels.

And here is Tolkien's description of Frodo encountering Lothlórien, the heart of enchantment in Middle-earth, personified by Galadriel:

> it seemed to him that he had stepped over a bridge of time into a corner of the Elder Days, and was now walking in a world that was no more… Frodo stood still, hearing far off great seas upon beaches that had long ago been washed away, and sea-birds crying whose race had perished from the earth… [Galadriel] seemed to him… present and yet remote, a living vision of that which has already been left far behind by the flowing streams of Time.

Fermor perceives a future and Frodo a past, but in both tellings a world which, in the usual perspective, either has not yet happened or is long gone, is, from another point of view, nonetheless still happening now. And not, of course, any old world but one suffused with unfathomable and emotionally charged meaning. (Both also start with a bridge, the significance of which we shall touch on in a moment.)

In trying to understand this matter a bit better, we might draw upon Australian indigenous philosophy. What has come to be called the Dreaming is non-linear, the very contrary of an arrow of time speeding in one direction from the past through the present into the future. Instead, it is oriented to origins which then unfold in a kind of continuous present, enduring after they have passed away when viewed linearly. In which case our joys, in a profound although no necessarily accessible way, are still happening, and nothing temporal, whether before or after, can change that.

Magic vs Enchantment

Where enchantment is about wonder, magic properly so called is about will: directing processes in the world, others and/or the self. This is the case even if those processes aim at changing one's consciousness, say. Historically, the figure of the male magus, using his arcane knowledge to manipulate unseen forces and bring about changes amazing to the ignorant masses, figured importantly in the formation of modern science. Indeed, we could say that science is "our" magic. Its wizards may wear white coats and work their magic in labs, but the underlying mode remains the same.

Science never rejected the occult – literally, what is hidden. Instead, led by Newton, it redefined it as of two kinds. One is occult forces which can be empirically observed, and these it claimed as its own. The other kind, which cannot be measured, it disowned. So astrology, for example, was dismembered. Lunar tides became part of science, but divination from a birthchart was rejected as impossible.

Modern science is a very important part of the project of modernity, namely the rational pursuit of mastery, including self-mastery. Since enchantment cannot be mastered and isn't interested in being master, it just gets bored and wanders off to look for something better. This is often what remains, in our globalised new world, of indigenous ways of life, whether traditional or relearned, in which concrete magic is the norm. These can also still be found in the modern world in what remains of wild nature; in the arts, when they have not been completely commodified; in religion, especially ritual, when it has not been perverted by politics; in scientific inquiry, when it has not been enslaved to industrial technoscience; and with those we love, whether human or otherwise.

So the world is not altogether disenchanted. Indeed, it never can be. Enchantment is a potential inherent in embodied beings in convivial relationships with many kinds of others – your 'countless soul', as the writer Judy Kravis puts it. That is why its possibility can never finally be denied. As such, it is a standing reminder (which is not always welcome) of the inherent limits of the modern project. Indeed, I believe that even in hostile circumstances, it continues to live in our bodyminds, awaiting only an awakening touch. Enchantment reawakens us to our common aboriginal condition, in the deepest and truest sense. It is a return and a remembering.

In a Song

Enchantment is personal. This is reflected in the word itself, which comes from the Latin verb *cantare,* to sing, plus the preposition *en*, in, which became the Old French *enchantement,* which then passed into Middle English. It thus means the experience of being, or finding oneself, in a song. Whether it is a song that one hears or that one is singing, one finds oneself both listening to it and experiencing it from the inside. The song can be any narrative, whether heard, read, seen or imagined. But you have to be there, participating. Staying on the outside, looking or listening in, won't suffice. (Nor will 'suspending disbelief'. If you have to do that, the enchantment has already failed.)

Another of Tolkien's definitions of enchantment is 'the realisation of imagined wonder': finding yourself in a real story, or storied reality, that you had only ever imagined. That can tip one into a state, and world, of wonder. As the poet Wallace Stevens says, 'In the presence of extraordinary actuality, consciousness takes the place of imagination'.

This is strikingly true of another kind of enchantment, when the cosmos inexplicably but unmistakably addresses a deeply personal issue. Formal practices of divination try to encourage and invite just that. And it is indeed possible to do so, although the connection which enchantment accompanies cannot finally be created or arranged. An example: on a fair day in early autumn, a friend was walking in a London park, oppressed by her approaching fiftieth birthday and, it seemed, old age, when she saw a bright turquoise-blue balloon floating high overhead before disappearing into the distance. A while later, she noticed it again, now floating on the edge of a pond. Concerned that waterfowl might become entangled in the trailing string, she managed to retrieve it, and turning it around, she found on it the words, 'Happy 50th Birthday!'

Like a bore at a party, there will always be those who cry 'Coincidence!' Since their default assumption is that the cosmos is fundamentally meaningless – and how would you scientifically test that hypothesis? – it seems only fair to ask in return, *cui bono*? Who benefits from saying so? Not the doubter, who merely fortifies his or her nervous orthodoxy and trades wonder for a trammelled sense of security. Not the person in question, for at such moments one feels, because one *is*, extraordinarily alive. The precise arrangement of unique moment and place (never merely time and space) is inherently and profoundly meaningful. As the anthropologist Lucien Lévy-Bruhl says, 'There is nothing further to seek when the myth has spoken'.

Indeed, we might say that one then finds oneself living mythically – that is, living in, and out of, the oldest narratives available to us. Such times in our lives, brief but momentous, are therefore fateful. Even to reject the enchantment – always possible in principle, however difficult in practice – is itself a fateful act. For this reason, too, the modern definition of myth as falsehood is itself a mythical claim, made under the aegis of Apollo, the god of reason.

Hermes

Myth contains millennia of accumulated human experience, including hard-won wisdom about it, in condensed and intensified form. Furthermore, since it is the experience and wisdom of Earthlings, mythic narratives ultimately comprise, in the words of the mythographer Sean Kane, 'the ideas and emotions of the Earth'. This is more obvious in what remains of the earliest myth, but even the humanoid divinities of Neolithic myth whom we know best remain, like the natural world, more-than-human. That is, they include but exceed humans and their traits. In this and other respects, gods and goddesses can be understood not only as figures but also as activities and qualities.

All enchantment is mythic, but not all mythic deities are enchanting. Far from it! So we shall concentrate on the two in the classical Greek pantheon who are most directly concerned with enchantment, namely Hermes and Aphrodite. Let's consider Hermes first. An ancient though youthful god, he was, and still is, the liminal god. (I first typed 'luminal', suggesting a light-bringer: a tiny example of something he often does.) As such, Hermes presides over thresholds (*limens* in Latin), and his office entails crossing them. That includes all ambiguous places which themselves cross and connect, such as doorways, staircases, corridors and especially bridges. (Plus, I would add, hotels and inns.) Sometimes new meetings result, other times unexpected messages which may be ambiguous or paradoxical; hence 'hermeneutics', the art of interpretation. By the same token, Hermes' formal job is psychopomp, bearing souls from one world to another. But he is not a heavyweight like Zeus and his brothers, being instead intensely light, quick and funny. Sexually, too, he is a male god but often with a female sensibility.

Hermes is present, then, in unexpected enchanting and enlivening encounters, especially where the parties come from different worlds and don't normally meet. But 'parties' extends beyond other humans to other animals, places, things and even ideas. Under Hermes' aegis, enchantment is indifferent to fretful modern strictures about what can and cannot have subjectivity or agency. The same applies to the logical rails on which modernity runs: x must only be x and nothing else, it cannot be both x and not-x, and it must be either x or not-x. (From Aristotelian logic to binary code is a short stretch.) Enchantment is hopelessly non-modern, so it ignores these so-called laws.

Metaphor

Nowhere is this truth clearer than in metaphor. The term itself means 'to carry across' from one domain to another, relating the two. Hence its affinity with Hermes. Something essential is shared, and that common ground is recognised, but without cancelling out differences. They remain but suddenly become less significant. Let me give you some examples of metaphor in action as enchantment.

Classically, there is the realisation that 'Achilles is a lion!' So Achilles is and is not (only) a man. At the same time, he also is and is not a lion. This tells us something absolutely essential about him, and the price of that insight – which modernists refuse to pay, thus losing the gift – is ambiguity and paradox, which often attends enchantment. Or one finds oneself enchanted by Broadway, say. So one is in Broadway and yet, at the same time and in the same place, in *Faërie*. You're still in Brooklyn – or Kansas, for that matter – but they are not. (This happened to Henry Miller. Luckily, since he was a novelist, we have a faithful account of it.)

Or to someone in the right circumstances, a certain woman, as may be, is evidently a goddess. But she doesn't thereby stop being a human woman. She is both, and heaven help you if you forget either one. Or take Father Christmas. As any sensible child knows (even if it completely defeats a certain famous Oxford professor), that red-suited, white-bearded man in the store both is and is not Father Christmas.

In literature, Homer's *Odyssey*, or Proust's *In Search of Lost Time*, or Tolkien's *The Lord of the Rings* are not just stories *about* a journey, or concepts then structured by the literary metaphor of one. Being completely inseparable from what they relate, and from the experience of reading them in which you end up somewhere else from where you started, or returned but now different, they are as much journeys as they are printed paper.

The logic of enchantment thus differs from the deductive logic that forms the basis of most of mathematics and the sciences. It aligns rather with metaphor as practised by religion, the arts and the humanities, when they haven't been otherwise co-opted. More importantly still, that is how we not only think creatively but live – not by ghostly abstraction but the green and gold logic of life. The pioneering thinker Gregory Bateson summarised it in what he calls 'the syllogism in grass':

We die.
Grass dies.
We are grass.

The fact that this is a logical fallacy (called 'affirming the consequent') pales into insignificance next to its profound truth. It is one recognised in the Bible – 'all flesh is as grass' – and in the equivalent literatures of every other religion. And the vegetable metaphor is integral to its truth. We and all living creatures are entirely dependent on the plant world and photosynthesis, which comprises by far the greater part of all biomass. Which brings us back to the Earthly origin and nature of enchantment. That existential truth is acknowledged by Greek myth in the primacy of the goddess Gaia, the first being to appear.

But Gaia herself was born out of the void. So that void was not – *is* not, since this is all still happening – a cold, nihilistic absence, a super-death to be feared and fled from. It is a fecund maternal potentiality, what that practical metaphysician who wrote the ancient wisdom text the *Daodejing* figures as 'the dark female'. It is she who gives birth to both men and women, and all the other 10,000 things. It is to her that enchantment ultimately leads, leaving us in awe at the extraordinary moment-after-moment birthing, and rebirthing, of everything that is and is not. In the midst of this vast creativity, all we can do is midwife. What higher honour is there?

3. Love

Here is the eighteen-year-old Alain-Fournier, in notes written immediately after encountering Yvonne de Quiérecourt, one year younger, on the steps outside the Grand Palais, Paris:

> … all of a sudden, there SHE is coming out opposite me, walking quickly, gazing resolutely in front of her. I whisper to myself: Fate! The whole of my fate … is entering the omnibus office [with her] – where is she going? … I can still see her broad-brimmed pink hat through the window – less clearly her blonde, childish, expressive head. And haughty with it all as if slightly confused, making her seem nevertheless slender and tall and evoking the effect of pretty things which pretty though they are fail to give any idea of the slenderness and elegance of a body beyond all dreams … and her unbelievable waist a tiny tear in the lower part of her brown skirt.

It is 1 June 1905. The following year she will marry someone else, and nine years later, after finishing his youthful masterpiece *Le Grand Meulnes* – a peerless account of adolescent enchantment and its end – he will die on the Western Front.

We are not exactly short of similar accounts, not to mention millions of popular songs. Another, by the crime novelist Margery Allingham, is fictional but its veracity is unmistakeable:

> Annabelle paused for a moment… Her hair spilt on to her tweed collar, her shoulders were tiny and rounded under the rough cloth, and her travelling bag was held behind

her in her gloved hand. For Richard she made one of those inexplicably momentous pictures, a pinpoint of wonder, gone as soon as it is born but not to be forgotten in a lifetime.

Presently … she made a little gesture of farewell and disappeared through the door in the wall, leaving him alarmingly bereft.

Women have been enchanted in love for as long and as deeply as men, of course. As the poet Ono no Komachi (*ca.* 850) puts it, with passionate precision, 'Even if I saw you/ only once,/ I would long for you/ through worlds,/worlds.'

All the principal dynamics of enchantment are present in such accounts: wonder and relationality, obviously, and fatefulness, and wildness. None of it has been, or could ever be, arranged, least of all its 'success'. There is also concrete magic, with the smallest 'physical' detail conveying unfathomable mystery. (By the way, although neither of these accounts is same-sex, there's no reason why they couldn't have been.)

Such enchantment cannot be reduced to sex, although that doesn't mean sexual love cannot powerfully enchant. It is one of the three great threshold experiences in human life (so Hermes attends all): being born, dying, and in-between, meeting another person in a way at once personally intimate and universal, even cosmic. Sex also places one within the great narrative of the creation of new life, whether or not conception ensues, just as the act of mating rehearses an ancient ritual. The effect is the enchantment that results from participating in something larger, older and deeper than oneself.

Needless to say, there are also profoundly disenchanting dangers, stemming from the cat's cradle of sex and power, that is, power-over, and in this case highly fraught issues of sex and gender. We shall return to them later. For now, as so often with anything important, the crucial thing is to hang on, defying contradiction, to both truths: love's deep, sweet enchantment and its devastating consequences when disenchanted.

As the two examples I've just quoted imply, romantic love is potentially even stronger. It may or may not include sex but in any case, there is nothing generic about it. It is all and only about this unique and irreplaceable person, so their concreteness becomes even more 'magic'. This is true even of fleeting encounters. A face seen passing in the street or on a train can spoil your whole day – '*O toi que j'eusse aimeé*' ('O you whom I would have loved': a line by Baudelaire) – but it holds good in sustained encounters too. And why fated? Because as Weber says, sounding like he speaks from experience, 'No consummated erotic communion will know itself to be founded in any way other than through a mysterious destination for one another: fate, in the highest sense of this word.'

In one of those paradoxes which often accompany enchantment, the deeper and more emotionally one apprehends a particular person, the more universal the quality. In this way, romantic love is a kind of paradigm of enchantment. As such, it can obscure other kinds: the love between parents and children – so me, yet not me! – and between friends: such sustaining common ground, despite the differences. It can even overshadow what, given skill and luck, it can mature into: a quiet fire, no longer leaping but glowing, quieter and more subtle, sweeter if less sharp.

Love is highly vulnerable to false enchantment. Here, Proust's anatomy of Swann in love is matchless, detailing, for example, Odette's spell and the terror thrown out from it, likely a murky halo, by the immense anguish of not knowing at every moment what she had been doing, of not possessing her everywhere and always!' He sums up this experience in perhaps the shortest sentence he ever wrote: 'One second later she had been gone for hours.'

Yet it is striking that when Swann once feebly tries to break Odette's power over him, exclaiming that she isn't even his 'type', Proust rebukes him for boorishness! Is he right, then, that to be enchanted by love, even when falsely, is more desirable and admirable than to be securely disenchanted? No one can say for sure, not even – or least of all – the person him- or herself. The answer depends on whom you're asking: the rational, self-possessed, apparently autonomous Swann or the besotted, emotional, deliriously happy or miserable Swann. There's no meta-Swann to adjudicate.

In which case, we may sensibly ask: who, of the selves in play, *wants* to escape? Another great account of enchantment in literature is *Death in Venice*, in which the learned Professor Aschenbach is completely captured by the 'god-like beauty' of the boy Tadzio. (The story was apparently inspired by arguably the wisest man in Europe, Goethe, in 1821, making a fool of himself at seventy-two with seventeen-year-old Ulrike Sophie von Levetzow.)

In any case, Swann and those in his position cannot reliably escape so easily. The counter-spell he attempts invokes the generic, abstract or universal against concrete magic, a classic ploy to gain mastery and control – this threatening whatever-it-is is a mere instance of a class of similar things – but it's no match for the goddess. (Scrooge tries the same tactic against the ghost of Old Marley – 'You may be an undigested bit of beef!' – but it doesn't work there, either.)

The temptation to cling becomes particularly strong when enchantment, even when true, withdraws. And sooner or later, it does. As the scholar and writer Roberto Calasso says, 'A god is never a constant presence.' One usually learns the hard way that trying to stop it only hastens the process. All you can do is keep the door open for a return, or a new presence.

Aphrodite

Given this intensity, it is unsurprising that love has mythic exemplars. In the classical Greek pantheon, it is Aphrodite, and she has much to teach us. An ancient and powerful goddess, there are no males, gods or otherwise, and few females, whom she cannot cause to fall in love. In the words of her devotee Sappho, 'Love makes me tremble yet again, sapping all the strength from my limbs. Bittersweet, undefeated creature – against you there is no defence'. Yet her greatest power is not to deliberately make anything happen but simply to emanate charm, delight and joy, the effects being what they may. Wherever and whenever these are happening, she is present.

Like all enchantment, Aphrodite's love promiscuously blends what an anxious modernity, like its religious forebears, tries to keep chastely apart: physical and spiritual, natural and cultural, 'high' and 'low'. She is a nature goddess, associated with doves, apples, roses, pearls and the Sun (more than the Moon). Equally, however, she brings refinement, adornment and art in all senses of the word, and for all the senses. Her erotic arts are both sensual and culturally refined, civilised and civilising, a rightful part of any adequate education. 'Golden' is her most frequent epithet, which unpacks into a rich array of meanings: gold itself, and therefore wealth and value, the Sun and light, pleasing and amusing speech, honey, and sexual fluids. Aphrodite is at once animal (the urge to copulate), mortal (in human form) and divine (a goddess).

Also like other enchantments, her love, and the wonder and awe it inspires, inheres in concrete magic. Her Greek honorifics include Aphrodite of the Little Ears and of the Beautiful Bottom. This is only scandalous for those keen to preserve the privileges of human over animal and mind over body, as if these could ever really be separated. Who we are as persons, including our most personal and spiritual selves, is bound up with our bodies and, through our bodies, the entire natural world. We are the scientific animal, the artistic animal, the religious animal. As Montaigne points out, 'upon the highest throne in the world, we are seated still upon our arses' – and without, he argues, any loss of dignity thereby. 'Our dignity,' as the philosopher Martha Nussbaum puts it, 'just is the dignity of a certain sort of animal'. It follows that we also suffer the indignities of animals. Even the sexual act, cosmic though it may be, is equally comic. Luckily, Aphrodite likes to play and laugh, so it helps if we can too.

Indeed, in so far as human beings are one kind of animal among many others, and fully as dependent upon the Earth, the narrative is ecological: a story that includes all of us but is greater still, and therefore correspondingly more potentially enchanting.

Aphrodite is also known as She Who Joins, Who Contrives and Who Turns Our Hearts, the Comforter, and the Postponer of Old Age. Both inside and outside marriage, she loves openly.

She is not neurotic, conflicted or ambivalent about it. Generous and unashamed, she doesn't hesitate to take the initiative in sexual relations. Yet here is nothing merely crude. Her carnality opens the door to a spiritual experience that transcends the flesh but is inseparable from it, one that hallows and is hallowed by it.

Hence the particular venom reserved for her worship by the early Church Fathers. They claimed to offer instead a spiritual love untarnished by any mere things, including bodies, and one that doesn't pass away. We shall look into this later in relation to religion. For now, it is true that in the words of the psychomythographer Ginette Paris, 'Love gives itself as eternal and departs; that is part of Aphrodite's myth'.

Monotheistic distrust of enchantment, which has passed into modern scientific attitudes, is highly gendered. One of its dictionary definitions is 'Alluring or overpowering charm, enraptured condition; (delusive) appearance of beauty', and the person casting such spells is invariably an enchantress, often described as a sorceress or seductress. This seems to be a peculiarly male fear, and the disenchanting demand which we allow it to give rise to is for truth that is universal (the only one of its kind), unchanging (context-free), and incontrovertible. Otherwise there is indeed a chance of being deluded, or at least mistaken – but that is the price for any enchantment at all. William Blake was right: 'There is a Smile of Love/ And there is a Smile of Deceit/ And there is a Smile of Smiles/ In which these two Smiles meet'.

Robert Louis Stevenson, lamenting their ephemerality, asks what has become of great, forever undying loves a generation or two later. Only, he answers, 'a few songs in a bygone taste, a few actions worth remembering, and a few children who have retained some happy stamp from the disposition of their parents'. Isn't such enchantment therefore hopelessly melancholic? It depends. If someone's being lovable is inextricably bound up with their uniqueness, contingency and vulnerability, then these cannot be separated.

After a certain age, at least, anyone who attempts to evade this paradox by chasing love itself, sacrificing any particular other, soon becomes mired in delusion and manipulation. (But this is not a moral judgement, unless in terms of the ethics of elfland.) Better is when the relationship modulates into one in which enchantment retains an honoured place. Even if it fails to do so, however, is the price of enchantment in suffering too high? That can only be answered by and for oneself. I would hope to pay willingly, even if not always gladly.

It might also be asked, why is the paradigmatic figure of enchanted love a woman, or a goddess? (It is certainly not a cyborg.) I have already suggested one reason, borrowed from the author of the *Daodejing*: the maternal and therefore female matrix of all life. 'The life-force of the valley never dies – this is called the dark female. The gateway of the dark female – this is called the root of the world'.

More tangibly, there is the female affinity with relationship as such, for example – as much significant symbol as biological cause – the potential to bear children that is woman's alone. From conception on, it is already multiple: a mother, a child and the connection between them. In addition, there is her intimacy with the child – who remains simultaneously an independent being and a part of her – and with still another person, the man who is a necessary part of the start of that process, and usually for long after, and who is not only a different individual but differently sexed. Thus femaleness can include men in a way that doesn't often obtain the other way round. Starting with the figure, activity or quality of a man (or god) would not take us to the same inclusive place.

By the same token, Aphrodite symbolises sexual and romantic love between people, regardless of whether they are men or women. Love is a relationship and its quality; it doesn't dictate who the parties are, or their sex.

Interdependence

The relational dynamics of enchanted love include but extend beyond sexuality. For example, regardless of their sex, at any given time one party is usually more active, while the other is more receptive or responsive (but not necessarily passive). The giver is sometimes identified as a male role and the receiver as female, but any real and rich relationship involves alternation between them. Both dynamics are paradoxical: true giving requires receiving the permission or blessing of the other person, while true receiving cannot take place unless one actively gives oneself to the other. Furthermore, the feminine party, although she or he invites the other in, is not therefore submissive; she can be the one in charge. Similarly, the masculine party, although he does indeed advance and perhaps penetrate, is not therefore dominant; he can be the one led.

Relationality is precisely not a thing; in between, the gap where enchantment lives, has no location or duration. In practice it is thoroughly embodied, however, and our bodies, in their concreteness, are a part of the natural world. Through them, we are embedded in, and connected to, the rest of it. (This is the essence of ecology, of course.) So women are not more interdependent than men but they do tend, for reasons of accumulated life experience, to be more aware of it. Another asymmetry between women and men, in heterosexual relations, tends the same way: being the ones who may become pregnant, with all that that entails, the potential consequences of sexual love are graver for women. There is more at stake.

In this light, men are relational and interdependent beings who are relatively and precariously more autonomous – although often paid for in the coin of alienation – and sometimes inauthentically or delusionally autonomous: that is, thinking and behaving as though they are independent when they aren't, and in denial about that fact. In fact, a degree of alienation – what has been called 'the male wound' – is built into human development, which is also asymmetrical respecting the primary early parent. (That would be the one with breast milk, unless something has gone badly wrong. Which is not to deny that it sometimes does, and must be fixed as best it can.)

The reason is that girls can more easily identify with their mother, or if not, then at least their mother's sex. Boys, however, must break away from both her and her kind in order to establish themselves as male. While female bodies exist in continuity, male bodies stand in contrast with the kind of embodied life that is their source but isn't them. The move into male independence is therefore fraught and provisional. It also means that men, feeling themselves to be outside or apart from the world, are predisposed to treat it a set of items, objects to be manipulated.

All this has profound implications for men's relationships with enchantment, particularly love. Finding themselves outside the feminine source of life gives rise to a kind of existential insecurity which often impels a desire for control. The strategies that result mitigate against receptivity to enchantment, but they also make the experience all the more powerful when it does happen. I think this is the reason why falling in love often hits a man so hard, 'with the comprehensive force', as Clive James puts it, 'of a revelation'.

I recently saw Edvard Munch's *Madonna* (1895/1902) for the first time. (I mean the actual painting, which should not be confused, as art so often is, with its reproductions.) It expresses everything that men, at some deep level, can feel about women: unreachable yet inescapable, erotic but ethereal, the one who birthed him and who will also see him out. Her face is equally Madonna, Magdalene and Pietà.

An asymmetry between men and women thus obtains, both in terms of our psychosexual development and metaphysically, as the female root of the world. Hence the mythic ascendancy of Aphrodite over both enchantment and femininity as such. But where does this leave men, apart from being included (although often feeling excluded)? I think it gives us a picture of masculinity as magnificent in its own way but touched with pathos: both powerful and vulnerable, with each aspect limiting and qualifying the other. Men embody an unstable amalgam of ruthlessness, from the developmental impetus to break away and confront, comradeship – the band of brothers, pals and desperados, living outside the law of life – and dizzying, breathless enchantment when it happens. As a result, many men spend a lot of time and energy either fleeing the dark female or chasing her, trying to get back in.

By the same token, men are particularly prone to attacks of sexual self-pity, which can turn rancid and dangerous when they blame women for withholding the connection (as it may feel) to life. Witness the 'Incel' movement, whose members believe they have a right to sex, which women apparently have no right to withhold. So far as I know, there's no female equivalent.

It's no surprise, then, that among the effects of strongly male-centred cultures and religions, obsessed with controlling women and sexuality, is the violent suppression of wild enchantment in love. Another factor is probably the need to promote marriage as an institution cementing social arrangements of power. In any case, the contrast with enchantment – the unbiddable effect of a spontaneously formed relationship across otherwise unbridgeable gulfs of all kinds – could hardly be clearer. Enchanted love is given freely or not at all. Whatever else it may suffer, it cannot be commanded.

A plethora of problems attending false enchantment awaits unwary lovers and partners. The most obvious is trying to possess and control the other. Then there is trying to recapture by will what is felt to be slipping away ('the thrill is gone', in the words of the blues song), or trying to prevent it doing so. That is a mistake which can also be repeated by replacing partners with new ones in the same vain attempt. The ultimate model for false enchantment, in love as elsewhere, is addiction.

Enchantment in other kinds of relationship presents its own challenges. With one's parents and children, assuming relations are not completely dysfunctional, one must learn to hold the affection and the frustration in delicate balance, recognising both as valid. And, even more fundamentally, to recognise them as both oneself and as other, as themselves. Too much of the first leads to overcontrolling, while too much of the second can be alienating. Both extremes disenchant.

Friendship offers deep and rich enchantment, sometimes obscured, as I said, by the dazzle of romance. But master the art of not having to dominate, and the wonder of two lives running alongside each other, nourishing each other without being asked, let alone forced, to do anything for the other, can last a lifetime. Sometimes, too, again with luck as well as skill, romantic love becomes a special kind of friendship for which there is no term or category. The result, in its deep and knowing affection, is often closer to the relatively selfless delight of true enchantment than when sexual desire is driven by passionate possession.

Control

The issue of control at the expense of genuine relationship, with its inherent wildness and risk, figures importantly in the modern programme to disenchant love by putting it through the mincer of evolutionary psychology and behavioural genetics. It's not that those sciences have nothing to say, but too often they are given the final word. No matter how fine-grained its analysis in terms of histocompatibility, oxytocin receptors, the amygdala, opposite-sex parent resemblance, reward mechanisms and all the other instruments in the current scientific armoury, enchantment as a first-person experience remains uncaptured, and it is base economy with the truth to pretend otherwise.

So why do they try? Nietzsche asks rhetorically, 'Isn't our need for knowledge' – our need, note, not the knowledge itself – a 'need for the familiar, the will to uncover, under everything strange, unusual and questionable, something that no longer disturbs us?' When this is the driving force, it's a quest for security, for mastery over a mystery. But a mystery properly so-called isn't something that can be 'solved', like a puzzle. It only gets deeper the more you look into it. Such depth is part and parcel of the beloved's concrete particularity; so reducing them, along with all enchanting others, to generic average types is first to disenchant, then claim you have 'explained' them. (As if that amounted, in any case, to understanding!)

Such a programme is nothing new. Its roots, at least, lie in Plato, who feared and therefore disliked love as concrete magic on account of its earthiness, fragility, risk of deception, inevitable passing and unpredictable return. He left us with an abstract idea of perfect Beauty uncontaminated by anything beautiful, and of Truth that is pure and unchanging because there is nothing and no one left to defile it by actually existing. Earthly love was instrumental, acceptable only as an enticement to higher spiritual states.

This poison passed directly into the bloodstream of Christianity and thence, Islam – not unmixed obviously, but virulent nonetheless. Thus we have womanhood exalted on condition of being utterly non-sexual (and even that is usually too much for Protestantism), while in orthodox Islam, piety for a woman is equated with her effective disappearance behind *niqab*, *burqa* and *chador*. In relation to enchantment, that is as obscene as its opposite and equally disenchanted extreme, pornographic sexualisation. Compulsion of any kind, whether gross or subtle, severely disenchants.

There are cultures of male domination with other historical roots, of course, and religious oppression of women continues, monotheistic and otherwise. It has now been joined by a secular and materialist version, however, which extends to fantasizing about taking control of the maternal function altogether, replacing it with scientifically controlled and adjusted reproduction. In its way, this would be the apotheosis of Plato's dream of self-created male souls, leaving behind women, the natural body and the 'surly limits' of the Earth.

It would also be the ultimate disenchantment of love. Love is not a ladder. It is, in the words of one of its chroniclers, Gabriel García Márquez, 'a state of grace: not the means to anything but the alpha and omega, an end in itself'.

Men, Women and Enchantment

We have found that compared with men, women have a more direct affinity with enchantment. Taken together with some of its most distinctive aspects, we can say that there is something distinctively female about it. An obvious contrast is the way the male wound, resulting from men's particular psychosexual development, leaves them in a more complex and ambiguous situation. This doesn't mean men can't be enchanted or 'do' enchantment; just that when they do, it is often in a female mode, or in ways that honour femaleness.

We have also seen that despite all their intractable problems, relationships between men and women can entail profound enchantment. That is hardly surprising – or else very lucky – since we are all usually born either male or female. These are not discrete essences, to be sure, but modes or ways of being, each one recursively defining, and defined by, its opposite. So there is a polarity, but it includes a continuum of ways each pole can be expressed or combined, and by whom. This is what 'gender' means, as opposed to one's biological sex.

There are serious issues about who gets to define – who has the power to define – what it means to be a woman or feminine and a man or masculine, and there is often destructive fallout from the effects of fearful, rigid or authoritarian definitions. Subverting gender enforcement, and lightening and loosening up, is all to the good. Lately, such challenges have been strengthened by an increased awareness of people born 'intersexed', that is, with some mixture of female and male sexual characteristics. The proportion is tiny but the phenomenon is real. There is also more awareness of those who feel that they have been born in a wrongly sexed body. Although that way of putting it skews the issue, suggesting that one's identity could ever be entirely separate from one's bodymind, the reality of the experience cannot be doubted. What then are the implications in this context?

None of what I've just discussed offers anything more than variations on the theme of sexual difference. There is no need to defend enchantment here, because our formative origins as a dimorphic sexual animal, and those dynamics, remain. More worrying is what seems to be an attempt to deny the reality of sexual difference altogether.

This is wrong and damaging, not least to the possibility of enchantment. No matter how complex and contradictory their expression, biological sexual differences entail certain characteristics, qualities and limits which cannot be altogether transcended or abandoned. Of course no one should be wholly defined by their anatomy or limited by their sexuality. But there is a lot to be said for owning part of who you are, and no mean part at that. No being is universal or infinitely plastic; to be at all is already to be particular.

To believe that one can be just whoever or whatever one chooses to be thus attempts to reject the embodied, embedded and ecological dimensions of our nature, all of which entail limits. That gesture disrespects and damages who we actually are, as well as the wonder that arises from being alive as who we are.

Limits these days have a bad press. I've lost count of the advertisements I have seen selling a product that will supposedly enable you to live 'a life without limits', or words to that effect. But limits are absolutely unavoidable, and necessary; they enable as well as constrain. Without them we would not only expire immediately, we would be unable to do anything at all. So whence this reckless and childish attempt to get rid of them, in so many contexts, which has become central to the modern project of self-mastery? I see a desire for certainty and lust for security at all costs, and those costs often include enchantment.

To be clear, I am talking not about this or that individual, whether one who finds sex-change liberating or one for whom it turns out to be a tragic mistake. My concern is with a movement or programme which is aimed at ultimately bringing the body entirely under control of the mind. Enchantment may well transgress, and often does, but it does so spontaneously. Deliberate or programmatic transgression is just another disenchanted rational programme. As such, it is easily coopted by modernity, so it won't be long before it is packaged and sold as a product, part of a lifestyle. By then, unchecked, it will have already become a counter-orthodoxy and a bore.

Such a movement aligns itself with the Promethean project of human self-mastery, whose provenance is thoroughly androcentric (male-centred) and belongs with the compulsively destructive 'move fast and break things' ethos of Silicon Valley and the so-called alt-right. In addition to the right not to be bullied for one's opinion, it would throw away feminism's hard-won recognition of the distinctiveness, value and glory of women as such, something that helps and heals us all.

We should therefore defend – indeed, celebrate – the reality and sometimes wonder of sexual difference. Then the focus can be where it belongs: on the kind and quality of relationships. (Inequality does not necessarily follow from difference, and the attempt to reduce the former by attacking the latter is seriously misguided. Inequality results from flawed relationships, not differences.)

Sexual difference is not the only kind of love that matters, of course, nor the only kind that offers enchantment. For example, what I've said has no implications, so far as I know, for sexual preference or choice of partner. But the differences between men and women are a particularly powerful source.

4. Art

Art is one of the principal sources of enchantment in many lives, and my own experiences in this respect are far from unusual. My attention, for example, has been captured by a landscape painting, looking not at but into it, as time slows until other viewers flicker around the edges and disappear like figures in a speeded-up film. Have I lost myself in it? But I find myself there, standing near those trees, seeing those distant mountains from within the frame. Have I then found myself in it? But I also remain in the gallery, in that city, on that afternoon. Or transported by music – an oboe, say, or a guitar solo – heard within myself although played without, to a different time and place which is somehow at the heart of where I am. Or rapt in reading, in the story, as the words – printed ink on paper – come to life in my mind, turning the page to find out what is going to happen to me next even as I sit in a room, holding a book.

There are ways to accommodate this sort of artistic enchantment and ways to discourage it, ways of thinking that allow it to be and others that obliterate it, sometimes in order to say it never happened. Chief among the former ways is Keats's negative capability, allowing the enchanting other to be whoever or whatever they seem to be. Which is to say, in effect, who or what, at that moment, they actually are.

Chief among the second kind of way is the question, 'Is this, or was this, real or imaginary?' Or to quote the commentary on an Ice Age carving of a female figure in a recent exhibition at the British Museum (and I'm not making this up): 'Was this a real goddess or a spiritual one?' Which is exactly the wrong sort of question to ask, as if reality and spirituality were mutually exclusive categories

– even where goddesses are concerned! – so the figurine couldn't possibly be both.

This sort of question is egregiously inappropriate – oh, let's not mince words: stupid –because everything is real and everything is imagined, so there can be no correct answer; and it is destructive because as Weber says, 'rationalisation and intellectualisation' is the classic means of disenchantment. Working *with* wild experience in dialogue with concepts is one thing, and can lead to genuine discovery. Subordinating it to a predetermined schema, where the answers have already been decided, cannot. With the latter, the demand for security and mastery seizes on whatever can be used to those ends and condemns anything else as mystical, impractical and above all unreal.

That is the death of concrete magic, which is why the great psychoanalyst D.W. Winnicott argues that the ambiguity of what he called 'transitional objects' – soft toys and so forth, to which children are passionately attached – should be accepted and respected. They both are and are not the child's self. 'By flight to split-off intellectual functioning,' he writes, 'it is possible to resolve the paradox, but the price of this is the loss of the value of the paradox itself.' Which is to say, you lose the metaphor and with it, any enchantment and its truth.

Equally disenchanting is forcing art to answer the question, 'What use are you?' Thus art is asked to pay its way, make money, advance a career or have certain social or political effects. All these things may happen, but if you want enchantment then they must follow, not lead. If art is not ultimately practised and appreciated for its own sake, the door is closed on its intrinsic value, which is what enchantment depends upon and reveals. To be sure, great art created for other purposes can transcend them. If you want to encourage enchantment in art, though, you will avoid making such demands.

This does not mean art is separate from or opposed to life. However wonderful, art is only one part of life. It is rooted in and depends on being alive, where the reverse is not true. (Unless, that is, you expand the meaning of 'art' until it comes to mean everything, and therefore nothing.) By the same token, art is a very particular kind of pursuit. What of the kind of enchantment it offers, then? For art is odd indeed. On the one hand, it doesn't merely represent things 'in the world' which are more real. On the other, artistic things are not wholly different or unrelated to things 'in the world'. How could they be? So art *presents* things, which then join the ranks of already existing real things. It does so by creative processes which add to, while partaking of, the creative processes of life itself.

In another remarkable twist, art can enchant when life (that is, the rest of life) does not. C.S. Lewis records that when he was a young child, his brother showed him a biscuit tin covered with moss, twigs and flowers, and 'What the real garden had failed to do, the toy garden did. It made me aware of nature… as something cool, dewy, fresh, exuberant.' Here is one of the chief dynamics of enchantment at work which we identified earlier, namely metaphor: the toy garden both is and is not a 'real' garden. In just such a way, a painted tree is and is not a 'real' one, a fictional person is and is not a 'real' one, and so on.

This metaphoric dynamic is as old and as fresh as art itself. The extraordinary scenes in the caves at Chauvet, painted more than 30,000 years ago, re-present the lions, horses, rhinos and other animals of the time with startling immediacy. They are alive, in all their stink and sheen and jostle. Yet from another perspective, we are looking at rock, charcoal lines and pigment. In the metaphorical place of these animals-who-are-not-animals – for anyone intelligent enough not to insist: well, which are they? – enchantment flourishes. Indeed, it may be more easily accessible than that of 'real' animals, whose metaphoricity can be harder to grasp. This is weird but nothing to be ashamed of; we are strange animals.

Hermes Again

Earlier we identified Hermes as the mythological exemplar of some of the dynamics of enchantment: boundaries and the crossing of them, liminal places and ambiguous messages, for example. We can further specify that role in relation to art. While still very young, Hermes famously encountered a tortoise and killed it without compunction to make a lyre, the first musical instrument. Thus we could say that he invented, or discovered, music.

There is a kind of ruthlessness about being an artist, although it differs from that of a warrior. Artists are not averse to sacrificing relationships, or using others as material, even when enchantment is what is sought. Often they are willing to steal others' time, too. Perhaps that is understandable, if not always forgivable; even the most privileged artists must fight to claw back time to work from the insatiable maw of daily life. Conversely, no small part of what gives their work its precious quality is the sacrifice of all the things they could, and maybe even should, have been doing instead.

Hermes is not a major player, however. He makes a point of evading direct power, preferring craftiness, agility and subversion. He is also no philosopher in the usual sense. Hermes doesn't observe, analyse or describe but intervenes; he persuades, seduces, beckons and reframes. This places him – and by implication, enchantment itself, including that of art – outside the dominant tradition of Western philosophy, 'rotten with perfection' of *logos*: mind (over body), spirit (over matter) and male (over female). Indeed, as I said earlier, Hermes is a male god but manifests a female awareness. He and Aphrodite are closer, and were more often worshipped together, than any two other classical deities.

Concrete magic, the amalgam of spirit and matter, is as crucial for enchantment in art as in every other walk of life. Accordingly, every art is realised – that is, becomes real, both in its accomplishment by the artist and its apprehension by an audience – through the senses. I don't mean the senses as 'purely physical' (whatever that means) but as what informs embodied subjectivity.

Stories

Where does this leave literature, in which the senses seem at one remove? Reading has never strayed very far from hearing, and psychic analogues of all the senses are potentially involved when one reads. In addition, another one comes into play: the sense of self-and-other (self vs other, self as other, other as self) as it develops through narrative time. You are and are not this other whom you are reading about, or rather, whose life you are inhabiting. You are reading the book but you are also in the book.

Another kind of metaphor by which literature enchants is narrative time itself, which you experience in the story. So it differs from clock time while you are reading, although it is not completely unrelated either, turning clock time into metaphoric time.

Not surprisingly, it is storytelling that most readily enchants. The sharpest contrast in fiction is the kind of realist literary novel which is concerned to show that we are all Grown-ups here. It does this by insistently self-conscious cleverness and irony. In the milieu of the urban literati, story-telling is often treated rather as an embarrassing elderly relative, someone to be tolerated but not encouraged. There are indeed still novelists who can tell a good story, but mostly it is pushed out into so-called genre fiction: fantasy, science fiction, crime, thrillers, historical novels, romances and epics.

Even there, it's not always safe. Take fantasy. After a brilliant start, Philip Pullman's trilogy *His Dark Materials* ends up hectoring. Ironically, that was just what C.S. Lewis, whom he dislikes so much, did at the end of the Narnia books, sacrificing the integrity of the story for Christian proselytising. The effects of Pullman's modernist virtue-signalling are a reminder that without a light touch, at least, story cannot survive programme. Regardless of the content – theism in Lewis's case, atheism in Pullman's – the result is disenchantment.

Enchantment survives in the Harry Potter series, because although Rowling has no interest in it (as compared to magic), she puts story first and marries it to developmental insight. In the *Game of Thrones* empire, however, it has been buried deep in gratuitous gore, salacious misogyny and cruelty disguised as 'realism'. (If there is some good reason why kindness, say, is less real than cruelty, I've yet to hear it.)

The work of the most enchanting storytellers exists at an oblique angle to the novel. The stories of Karen Blixen and Giuseppe di Lampedusa, Italo Calvino's early wondertales (before he contracted hypermodernitus), the novellas of Russell Hoban, John Crowley's fantasy masterpiece and 'magical realism' by Mikhail Bulgakov and Bruno Schulz, as well as Gabriel García Márquez, all come to mind. So does Proust's lifework. No less than Tolkien's epic quest, it is a kind of storytelling which goes back at least to Homer. (There is a metaphorically exact and equally enchanting cinematic equivalent of Proust, by the way – indeed, his work was one of its inspirations – namely the incomparable *Heimat* films of Edgar Reitz.)

Already in 1936, Walter Benjamin lamented that 'the art of storytelling is coming to an end. Less and less frequently do we encounter people with an ability to tell a tale properly. More and more often there is embarrassment all around when the wish to hear a story is expressed'. Why? Because 'the epic side of truth, wisdom, is dying out'. And, he added, 'The fairy tale, which to this day is the first tutor of children because it was the first tutor of mankind, secretly lives on in the story'. (Confirming Benjamin's point about wisdom, the film version of *The Lord of the Rings* could not tolerate personal wisdom or nobility of character. Anyone openly showing it in the books, such as Treebeard or Faramir, was made to look foolish and inept.)

Storytelling survives, however, because many people long for it. Tolkien is one of the greatest modern storytellers, and therefore also the butt of bitter critical contempt. As Auden (a lifelong admirer and defender of Tolkien's fiction) points out, 'the gift of mythopoeic imagination… is one with which criticism finds it hard to deal, for it seems to have no necessary connection with the gift of verbal expression or the power to structure experience'. But the problem runs deeper, because those critics who pride themselves on being Adult are actually cases of arrested development. They have stopped short of true maturity, which consists, in this context, of a 'second naïveté'. I mean a recovered sense of wonder, tested and tempered, on the far side of suspicion and critique. Many readers seem to be there already. Tolkien always insisted that 'the "fairy-story" is really an adult genre, and one for which a starving audience exists'. The sales figures alone, for such an extremely unlikely as well as long book, prove him right.

As for poetry, I think it offers the purest and most concentrated literary enchantment; indeed, too strong for many readers, who seem to prefer theirs with a little water, or a lot. But I probably quote more poets than any other profession, for the good reason that from long practice, they are often best able to articulate enchantment. A good poet is, as Richard Wilbur says, 'a scholar of the heart'. Poetry's contemporary problems – mainly from overly-intellectualised and self-conscious practitioners, many of them academically trained – do not detract from that description.

It's true that poetry's estate has fallen far. The poet, the seer and the philosopher were once almost identical, but who, of the great if not the good, listens now? Yet readers remain, even if we don't know them, and poetry's mantic reach can still unexpectedly encompass a hidden corner of the soul.

Recall Michael Longley's observation about writing a poem, that in order to release the subject's 'mysterious aura' you need to capture it with precision. The implications are much wider, of course. The mystery ('magic') exceeds the circumstances ('concrete') but doesn't exist apart from them, and it depends on their successful evocation.

D.H. Lawrence discussed poems in an equally resonant way. 'The essential quality of poetry,' he wrote, 'is that it makes a new effort of attention, and "discovers" a new world within the known world'. Such an effort requires an 'intrinsic naïveté without which no poetry can exist, not even the most sophisticated'. His own poems, in the stories they tell and the way they do so, exemplify that truth.

Metaphor and Wildness

Metaphoricity takes the etymology of *en-chant-ment,* being in a narrative, to a new level. It is at play not only in literary storytelling but in every art, each in its own way. In visual art, for example, without leaving the room one nonetheless finds oneself inside the picture – or fails to, in which case the enchantment fails too. This process is even stranger with music, which is arguably the most concrete – immediately and intimately sensuous – and mysterious – ineffable, intangible – of all the arts. Music is neither 'external' (a matter of acoustics) nor 'inner' (a question of psychology) but always inextricably both, and therefore neither alone. The wrong question here, therefore, is again: 'But which is it?'

That third thing, so to speak, is deeply metaphorical. Music involves notes in relationship to other notes, whether simultaneous, as harmony, or successive, as melody. I am speaking of music, not sound or noise. Music is a kind of sound, of course, but cannot be reduced to it. Nor, despite John Cage, is all noise potentially musical. (I cannot argue the case here, but Cage was a theory-driven modernist – Maoist in music as much as in politics – who set out to destroy it in much the same way as Duchamp did visual art.) Conversely, limits are essential to music, even, or especially, in the case of improvisation, one of its most powerfully enchanting forms. So when music tries to proceed without limits, as in 'free' music/jazz, it destroys itself as music, and with it, any enchantment.

By the same token, there must be gaps – silences in music, spaces in paintings – for art to enchant. If you fill every gap and space then metaphor, which crosses and connects, becomes impossible, and enchantment with it. Instead of being both in the art and outside it, the listener or viewer becomes either completely shut out or completely shut in. This is the effect of Mark Rothko's canvases, for example, and John Coltrane's 'sheets of sound'. They may be good, even great art in other respects, but the only enchantment leaks out of them incidentally, on account of some of the colours and notes. And it's not surprising. The tortured Rothko sought healing and perhaps salvation, and Coltrane, too, turned jazz into a vehicle for his religious fervour. Both reduce art to a means, and no matter how exalted the end, that suppresses enchantment.

By implication, the following predispose to enchantment, although they are far from the only ways, obviously: *gleaming, shimmering, glittering, dazzling* (but not blinding), visually; and *pulsating, ringing, resonating* (but not deafening), aurally. All involve oscillation back and forth across a gap.

A musical note is as far from a thing-in-itself as it's possible to get. Harmony is completely relational – what makes a note what it is is the other notes which it is not – while the essence of melody is motion: a succession of notes rising, falling, moving laterally or turning back upon itself, slowing, speeding up, and often ending up somewhere quite else. Its sense (or lack thereof) is also determined by the relationships between those notes, in this case in time. But exactly what is moving, and what kind of time is this? No-things, moving in a narrative time that they themselves create! The scope for enchantment is accordingly intense. Perhaps this is what the critic Walter Pater meant when he mused that 'All art constantly aspires towards the condition of music'.

As in its other sites, enchantment in art is wild and therefore unbiddable. This makes it radically different from wilful action, or knowledge as power, or any other exercise of power that attempts to control, manipulate or exploit. We might even say that it is what cannot be controlled. However, artists who want their art to enchant must exercise a great deal of effort, will and skill. The point is that their goal must not be to create or control enchantment itself, but rather to create and control the conditions it needs and likes, in the awareness that even the best possible ones cannot guarantee success. This attitude requires, and encourages, humility. It puts will at the service of wonder.

This is not to say that enchanting art is the only good kind. Out of many possible examples, Picasso's *Guernica* and its antecedents in Goya's portrayals of the horrors of war, Dylan's early anti-war songs and Brecht's bleak political plays are all superb art in their own way, which has nothing to do with enchantment. One *could* find any of these enchanting, to be sure, even if it's less likely. But if that happens, it will involve not enlightenment, nor moral outrage, nor an increased impetus to political activism, but simply wonder at the work. (Nothing annoyed Brecht more than audiences, including his own, 'who look at the stage as if in a trance, an expression which comes from the Middle Ages, the days of witches and priests'.

Treating art as use-less and price-less, in the strict sense, frees artists to concern themselves with its intrinsic value – the work's 'lining and depth' – which is what enchantment reveals. I shall let the writer Fernando Pessoa summarise a plethora of quotations on this theme: 'Why is art beautiful? Because it's useless. Why is life ugly? Because it's all aims, objectives and intentions. All of its roads are for going from one point to another'. As Wallace Stevens also remarks, a great deal of modern art 'has a reason for everything. Even the lack of reason becomes a reason.' (He was thinking of Surrealism, but the same is often true of abstract and conceptual art as well.)

Indeed, most of the art establishment – a cabal of celebrity artists, museum and gallery curators, corporate donors, modernist critics and art dealers – regards enchantment with contempt and is solely concerned with use and price. Purveyors to the 1% of what the critic Brian Sewell memorably termed 'shiny shit', their programme turns on the deliberate avoidance or destruction of intrinsic value in art, which would reduce its resistance to being commodified. Hence Dinos Chapman's brazen justification for defacing some etchings by Goya: 'You can't vandalise something by making it more expensive'. No, not if market value is the only kind you recognise.

In emphasising the uselessness of enchanting art, I don't mean to exclude crafts. In fact crafts are highly enchantment-friendly, because they require personal mastery (not systemic) and individual production (not industrial). They also involve an intense working relationship which is necessarily cooperative rather than domineering. The agency of the material, whether clay, wood, stone or whatever, must be respected. The resulting artefact usually can be used for something, of course, but that was not its sole purpose in being made. Nor does its owner usually relate to it as purely functional. Its aesthetic qualities are literally inseparable from its material form as a pot, utensil, jacket and so on, and this metaphorical marriage of practical and spiritual is itself enchanting.

Modern vs Modernist

Here I must register an important distinction, in relation to artistic enchantment, between 'modern' and 'modernism'. We are all modern in the sense of living in what are thought of as modern times, understood more as a certain sensibility than a period but beginning, very broadly speaking, with the advent of the twentieth century. But modernism, which I have just been describing, is an *attempt* to be modern, and in pursuit of this goal modernists seize on some modern concerns and tendencies and turn them into a programme. The modern desire to overtly innovate and experiment in relation to inherited traditions, for example, turns into iconoclasm: a systematic campaign not to revise or develop tradition but to destroy it and declare a cultural Year Zero.

The difference is clear enough if you compare, say, indisputably modern artists like Henri Matisse, Claude Debussy, Joseph Conrad and Wallace Stevens with modernists like Marcel Duchamp, Arnold Schoenberg, James Joyce and Ezra Pound. In jazz, the contrast can be supplied by thinking of Thelonious Monk, Bill Evans or Sonny Rollins, as against Cecil Taylor, Charlie Parker or John Coltrane. The moderns I just mentioned all honour enchantment in the work of their teachers and mentors, and try to pass it on in their own. The modernists, whether with icy Apollonian control or orgasmic Dionysian emotion, try to replace it.

So all works of art *can* enchant, but some are more enchanting than others. And when the unlikely ones do enchant, it takes a gentle revenge on them. Whether distant and cool or in-your-face and overwhelming – let's take Mondrian's abstract paintings and Wagner's operas as instances of each – and regardless of their creators' intentions, they become warm, intimate and personal.

In fact, what happens subverts both categories, modern and modernist alike; for the experience of enchantment is fundamentally *non*-modern. In that moment of rapt attention, taking deep delight in the other, all the issues of modernity, which so easily become a quest for mastery, absolute truth and freedom from limits, vanish. Since time is suspended, so is history, along with the effects of years of careful schooling. To modernists, who revel in difficulty for its own sake and rely on it to weed out the ignorant *hoi polloi*, this is appalling.

The work of Jeff Koons was a breakthrough, if you like, in welding together élitism and vulgar populism. The modernist critic Peter Schjeldahl, defending it, says: 'His majestic baubles are carefully empty-minded monuments of and to the global impunity of sheer wealth. To dismiss them, you'd need to get into a time machine and redirect the course of present history.' But that's exactly what enchantment does, although not in the way of a time machine, or any other kind. The root Indo-European word for 'machine' is the same as that for 'magic'. Both are powered by the will, and that's just what enchantment is not.

What happens in the moment of enchantment is that the work's historical provenance, cultural significance, its creator's psychology and social context and all the various movements and schools, fall away, even if they helped you into the frame. The point is not that the experience of enchantment is anti-intellectual, though, any more than it is anti-modern. It is simply non-intellectual, or non-analytical. This is true even when it has been precipitated (as it may be) by words and ideas.

Thus, wealthy vulgarists have taken over the art world, and according to their acolytes painting itself may now be hopelessly passé, and the subject matter may be superstitious or bourgeois, but right now you are in the landscape by Samuel Palmer that you are looking at. It is glowing with an inner light as you walk home from church under a huge Moon, and although the picture is tiny, there's lots of room in there.

The same thing could be extended to all the other arts. In music, for example, we see the global domination of an alliance between the corporate entertainment industry, partly exploiting and partly creating a vast popular market for bad music, and the unsleeping technological hyper-control that makes it technically possible. The result is profitable generic pap, written by marketing teams, delivered in interchangeable voices and poses, to be consumed like any other industrial product.

As the musician and critic Pierre Schaeffer notes, comparing now to the sublime time when the romance of the African-American blues and European classical music gave birth to jazz: 'decades later, this bloated, avaricious and barbarous culture, brutalised by money and machines and advertising, is still living off this precious vein. Well, you have to admit that some periods are simply vile, disgusting, and that this is one of them.'

Yet it is also true that no one could honestly say enchanting music is extinct. Like its Hermetic patron, it slips through the nets of commerce and fashion, popping up in this concert hall or that pub's back room, whether live or recorded, often thanks to musicians building up local and tribal followings through the internet and small gigs or just playing for and with friends. In the words of the pianist and writer Susan Tomes, 'music is a gift, even for the giver'. Enchantment is what happens when this fact comes alive and reminds us, in spite of everything, of its truth.

5. Religion

Religion is both one of our most potent means of enchantment and one of its chief enemies. Before unpicking this paradox, let's be clear what we are talking about. By 'religion', I mean a sustained relationship with the sacred, together with others, whether past or present, through practising certain rituals within particular traditions. This overlaps with 'spirituality' but is more collective and institutionalised, where spirituality is relatively informal and often more individual. And by 'the sacred' I mean ultimate value which is, in effect, final. Religion is thus a way of life, or part of a way of life. It is not a set of beliefs or propositions whose truth can be 'objectively' evaluated, scientifically or otherwise. Religious truth is personal, and it can only be tested by the difference it makes when it is taken up and lived.

How can religion be both enchanting and disenchanting? The answer lies in distinguishing between religious practices, on the one hand, and theology on the other. Every religion undertakes certain essential rituals – the Catholic Mass or Anglican Communion, Jewish Passover service, Muslim *Jum'ah*, Buddhist ceremony for taking refuge, Hindu *puja* and so on – in which celebrants honour, celebrate and partake of the sacred mystery at its heart. These often include a narrative dimension centred on the life of the founder, as well as of earlier celebrants.

The potential for enchantment is easy to see. Your relationship is affirmed with something that is much bigger, older and more important than yourself. It can be touched through symbolically enacting the appropriate story, and you thereby take your place in a community of like-minded others, both local and global as well as across time. 'To be in a song', in short. And what a song! But no matter how mighty it is, one is not thereby extinguished. It remains a relationship with an other who enchants – an other, maybe, who is the ultimate source of wonder.

At the level of doctrine, however, a religion's overriding concern is the state of your soul. In a word, is it saved (or some equivalent) or not? And such salvation is usually framed as permanent: once-for-all, or not at all. Thus, for example, Jesus says (in John 4:13–14) that 'whosoever drinketh of the water that I shall give him shall never thirst', while Buddhist orthodoxy exalts the extinction of the self, never to return to the cycle of worldly suffering. The contrast with enchantment could hardly be clearer. Its wonder ('magic') cannot be separated from this world ('concrete'). For the same reason, it always passes and must therefore, if possible, be renewed.

Official religion, and even its New Age versions, thus has a distinct purpose, and its guardians and experts are reluctant to rest content with letting you experience wonder as a result of its rituals. They want to tell you what it *means* and to control its meaning, trying to ensure that you draw the correct conclusions. Unlicensed enchantment is unwelcome, and often held in contempt as inferior, imperfect, merely Earthly and so on.

The result of this purposefulness, instrumentalism and orthodoxy is that no religion is without an equally powerful disenchanting imperative. The point to keep in mind, however, is that both impulses co-exist, each unevenly influencing the other but not altogether cancelling it out. At the vernacular level, however dismaying it may be for purists, most people are adept at drawing their own selective conclusions, bracketing unwelcome implications and ignoring contradictions, while availing themselves of the enchantment, among other things, that religious practice offers.

For Example

My own life experience in this domain might be instructive. I have had a longstanding (or -sitting) relationship with Zen Buddhism, beginning with hearing the Zen master Shunryu Suzuki teaching in San Francisco in 1970. A chance encounter, as we say in Middle-earth. I didn't really understand what he was talking about or even saying (his English was pretty poor), but I did know it was vitally important, and that I needed to find out more.

From the beginning, therefore, my involvement was led by relationship. This was reaffirmed when Suzuki's assistant at the time, Kobun Chino, became my teacher many years later. In 2000, I finally took my lay Buddhist vows with him present. It was a startlingly emotional experience – something to do with returning, or coming home – and at one point the image popped forcefully into my mind of the Return of the Prodigal Son. An image from my own culture, of course, and none the worse for that!

That emphasis has continued since Kobun's death in 2002. In addition to enduring friendships which began life at the small centre he started in Europe, I still go and see the woman who used to run it. Now in her eighties, she lives a reclusive life in a tiny Austrian village, and that's all most people seem to see. (Maybe it's because she doesn't shave her head and wear robes.)

Nonetheless, she is a dragon-spirited master who is intensely, if inwardly, engaged. I don't speak her language and she speaks little of mine, but every time we meet some kind of tacit transmission takes place. Her advice to me – 'Stay with your self' – 'Stay with *in* your self' – 'It is waiting for you' – sounds banal in cold print or merely odd, although less so in a world of addictive electronic distractions on top of all the usual ones. Coming from someone who actually practises this, however, it arrives with the clarity and authority of an old church bell struck just so, ringing with resonances of other teachers: Montaigne, Chu Hsi, F.M. Alexander… Sometimes I point these out but it always feels rather beside the point; it's not a seminar. (Oddly enough, I know another elderly dragon lady, wild and sharp and equally misunderestimated, in England. But that's another story.)

Wittgenstein, another such teacher, held that philosophy cannot tell us anything new but only remind us of something we already know. For example, 'the place to which I really have to go ne that I must actually be at already'. Rejecting a fundamental metaphor of Platonism – a ladder which one ascends in order to become divine – he adds that 'Anything that can be reached with a ladder does not interest me.' Indeed, all genuine spiritual teaching, it seems to me, is about remembering, recovering and returning to something so simple and ordinary that it's extremely difficult for us to access. And that is where enchantment lives. Even when the occasion is unusual, exotic or spectacular, its wonder is a reminder of our common condition: in the gutter, maybe, but looking at the stars.

This is not to say that doctrine is irrelevant, even in my own eclectic case. Both temperamentally and intellectually, I have never warmed to the idea of God, so I was already interested in Buddhism as a religion without that particular baggage. (That Buddhism *is* a religion, by the way, is something only a fool or ignoramus could deny.)

Throughout my years of practice, such as they are, I have struggled with what is officially the core practice of my religion: sitting meditation, or *zazen*. In a nutshell, I find it desperately disenchanting, a remorseless ongoing confrontation with pain and misery as per the Buddha's first Noble Truth that life entails suffering. At the same time, however, in the annual retreats, when *zazen* is inescapable, I find everything else we do – bowing and prostrations, offering incense, chanting sutras, the silent and delicately choreographed meals and intense work periods – pure concrete magic.

In fact, they seem to be just as 'core' as the meditation, and the combination a package that allows it all to work. Is it then a symbolic reminder of the dance of suffering and wonder that makes up life as a whole? Or of the fact that in order to have a healthy relationship with enchantment, one must be able to handle its absence? Both and more, probably. I only know that afterwards, I feel exhausted but winnowed and renewed.

If I am right, current attempts to modernise and secularise Buddhism, and the attendant industry of 'mindfulness', are an exercise in just the rationalisation that Weber identifies as the essence of disenchantment. They involve a simple-minded reduction of Buddhism to meditation alone, when it occupies a pretty marginal place in most traditional Buddhism, being left to monks when practised at all. Then there is a further drastic reduction of meditation itself to mindfulness alone.

Together, these facilitate the commodification of mindfulness as a lifestyle accessory. Mystery ('magic') is unwelcome, because how do you calculate it? So we'll get rid of the tiresome concreteness, dispose of the awkward particularities as mere tradition and superstition, and market what's left as a method. (I would add that if mindfulness is taken into workplaces and schools, it will of course become institutionalised in turn, with all that follows. It would be absurd to expect otherwise.)

My own small struggle is reflected in Buddhism as a whole. Its salvific focus is on attaining enlightenment, whether now or in a future life, but I'm sure its practitioners have a thousand and one takes on that which might not pass official muster. For example, in Zen Buddhism the technical meaning of the term *tathatā*, which is usually translated as 'suchness' or 'thusness', is something like the way things actually are – the true nature of things, whether anyone realises it or not.

Such objectivism is not only disenchanting but offhand about the participation that enchantment requires. However, the experts cannot stop it actually happening, and thereby becoming real, in and as someone's experience. In which case suchness, in all its concrete magic, could indeed manifest as wonder, even joy, at the mystery of how things are just now and here.

And Yet

The same tension plays out in Christianity and Islam, whose potential for disenchantment is unparalleled. As the first universal monotheistic religion, Christianity set this momentous ball rolling, with repercussions that assail us still. The aspect that most concerns us resonates with Weber's description of a fundamental prerequisite for disenchantment: 'the knowledge or belief... that one can, in principle, master all things by calculation'. That is what one true God, unlike many gods or none, supplies in spades: a master principle or truth against which everything can supposedly be measured, evaluated and ordered.

To that end, no rivals are permitted. A truth cannot be universal if there are other equally ultimate but perhaps contradictory truths, and it cannot be single if it doesn't hold sway everywhere and always. Thus monotheism is a standing invitation to imperium. This is expressed, for example, in the influential interpretation as *coge intrare* ('force them to enter') of Luke 14:23: 'Then the lord said unto the servant, "Go out into the highways and hedges, and compel them to come in, so that my house may be filled.' And rather less subtly in the *Qur'an*, surah 9, verse 5: 'Slay the polytheists wherever you find them'. Of course, there are countervailing tendencies, some with potential for enchantment, in both religions. It is delusory or dishonest, however, to pretend that there is no such problem.

Historically, the 'one God, one people, one land' of Deuteronomy, universalised by the early Christian church, merged easily with imperial power's 'one God, one empire, one emperor' well beyond the Roman Empire, directly informing Islamic militancy and eventually, suitably secularised, modern empires and movements. The model for modern revolutionary terror – not only French but Maoist, Cambodian and Iranian – was never far from hand. (The last three movements were directly and powerfully influenced by Western ideas, principally Marxism–Leninism, to which the same point applies.)

'The effort to identify the presumptively universally compelling Truth and Way and to compel it universally', in the words of the philosopher Barbara Herrnstein Smith, created and then stocked new categories of hate: infidel, heretic, apostate, idolater, unbeliever, heathen and pagan. That effort was fed by two powerful metaphysical injunctions with intensely practical effects. One is the Mosaic distinction, which impels the question: is this (whatever it may be) from and of the one God or not? The other is the Platonic distinction: is this universally true knowledge or false? These two imperatives then merged in Pauline and Augustinian Christianity.

The resulting logic remains untouched, and it is fatal for wild, multiplicitous, sensuous enchantment. Add the fact that the God of Christianity and Islam is spiritual as opposed to material, and male as opposed to female, and that effect is doubled by enmity to women, the body and the Earth – the common font of enchantment. The enmity breaks out into the open in Gnosticism, various Protestant sects, radical Islamism and modern scientism, but its potential never sleeps. Indeed, the last two count as enchantment's bitterest contemporary enemies, scientism for reasons that we shall discuss later and Islam on account of it being the purest monotheism, undiluted by a Trinity, reverence for the mother of God (in one of His three aspects), and any allowance for Caesar.

And yet, and yet… It's not that simple, of course. In the end, every religion is perforce a messy compromise between what of its orthodoxy can be enforced and what most of its followers want and need, which is often quite different. In their inchoate but determined pushback, room will be found for enchantment, even if constrained, in women's empowerment, communal solidarity, ritual wonder, fabulous stories, and spirit-beings whose good/evil status remains stubbornly ambiguous.

Even theologically, there are counter-currents. In Christianity, for example, there is the role of Mary. True, the price is high: desexualisation, and value by virtue of bearing a son, while even then it's an idol too far for most Protestants. But at least there is a way to licitly honour women. Nowhere is this more powerfully present than in Christian art (unlike that of Judaism or Islam), where it has largely escaped unscathed the effects of proselytisation. Then there is the Trinity, a unity-with-difference whose paradoxicality allows enchantment even if it passes most understanding (which may indeed be its point).

More poignantly, *caritas* – the love proclaimed by St Paul, to which differences between people are no obstacle – is tantalisingly close to the unpossessive love that we have identified as the essence of enchantment. That it must share space with pogroms, crusades and the Inquisition doesn't completely invalidate that proclamation, which has been taken up by many subsequent struggles for liberation. It is also a reminder that there are religious goods with little or no bearing on enchantment. Recent historical scholarship has shown beyond any reasonable doubt, for example, that secular human rights and the civil state alike have thoroughly Christian origins.

Above all, uniquely Christianity in major religions, there is the Incarnation, in which God, the most spiritual Being, becomes a vulnerable, limited human being. Allowing for theological qualifications (it's only happened once, it was a man, and so on), what could exceed the concrete magic, paradox and deep metaphor of a universal, transcendent, off-planet deity manifesting as a baby in a poor family, growing up into a man, and even being nailed to a cross? Christ as both human and divine is a tensive truth that is potentially powerfully enchanting.

Another reason why wonder survives and often flourishes in religions, even monotheistic ones, is that no one can actually live according to their dictates; not completely or for long. In practice, for example, I daresay no one relates to God, or *can*, purely as an 'I Am That I Am': Being, say, or the ground of Being, or universal love. We are non-self-identical, limited and interdependent beings, so any real relationship with God – which is to say, a god who is real for us – requires a particular, 'concrete' god.

Wonder also lives in the rituals. Mass and Communion can enchant its communities of participants through locating them in the central story of Christianity – the Incarnation, Crucifixion and Resurrection of Christ – through the concrete magic of its specifics, the wine and the wafer. In Anglican Christianity, the dominant religion in my part of the world, you don't need to be a 'believer' to be moved by a sense of continuity with many others who have stood in the same church, equally helpless in the face of death, or by the dignity of the Book of Common Prayer ('Earth to earth, ashes to ashes, dust to dust…').

Then there are countless more personal spiritual experiences, outside the net of formal religion but also inseparable from it.

In 1970, at San Francisco Zen Center, I attended my first week-long retreat. These feature a great deal of sitting meditation and some ritual, supported by just enough food to survive but not enough sleep. I had never experienced anything remotely like it and was soon in shock, edging towards despair.

Everyone was permitted one interview with the person leading the retreat, and when my turn came I was shown into a tiny room where the Zen master Dainin Katagiri – dark, intense, severe – was waiting. I sat down on the cushion opposite him, we bowed, and he looked closely at me for a moment before saying, 'OK, no questions. We just sit.' So we did, and I can only describe what happened next by saying that the room began to fill up with love: light, warm and wholly supportive, rising from the ground up like water, until it was full, and I was in it and it was in me. Then he opened his eyes and bowed again, signalling that the interview was over. Speechless, I bowed back, staggered to my feet and floated out the door. Thanks to that, I survived the retreat. I have never forgotten or stopped feeling grateful.

So is there a spiritual love, or power, which radiates universally and is at the heart of all religion? I only know that if there is, then it can't enchant, or do the work of enchantment, unless it acts locally, in particular circumstances, with actual people. Then it becomes real.

6. Food and Drink

A small boy I know (me, yet not me) used to await the annual harbinger of winter, a heavy plywood crate of tangerines, so he could be first to pick one out, remove its paper dress with the strange foreign words on it and carefully unpeel it, releasing tiny sparkles that promised what the first fat segment would deliver: a delicious explosion in my mouth of the far-distant South and Sun.

It's not really that much of a stretch from the enchantment of religion or spirituality to that of food and drink. I don't even need to invoke the obvious bridge of the sacraments. Both are utterly but not merely carnal experiences in, and of, precise circumstances featuring relationship. Both reveal metaphoric truths, and neither are biddable by our will alone. At the heart of Karen Blixen's exquisite short story *Babette's Feast* is an account of an understandable confusion between the two; the severely Protestant Jutland villagers, overwhelmed by the effects of Babette's French cuisine, attribute them directly to God. Only the general, a man of the world who once dined at the Café Anglais where Babette used to be the chef, understands what has happened.

Let's consider what nourishes us in its specifics. Although some of us easily forget it, food is something on which life depends absolutely. Properly understood, that fact alone is enough to permit enchantment. Food doesn't simply enable us to survive in the barest possible way, it also enables us to lead the fullest and finest lives. Furthermore, eating it is already relational: something that is not you becomes part of you. Being relational, that is, two-way, the counter-truth is also unavoidable. In a way not entirely captured by the crude slogan 'You are what you eat,' over time you are indeed strongly influenced by what you eat, as well as how you do so.

What exactly are we eating? Not only 'purely physical' properties (which is itself a metaphorical way of speaking), any more than we are 'purely physical' beings without subjectivity, agency or awareness. Rather, we are eating everything that went into that food, all the processes that made it, from the particular ground, with its soil and the weather there and then, to exactly what particular humans did with it. Like all enchantment, therefore, food is equally natural and cultural.

It is also concrete magic, both sensuously material and mysteriously meaningful: the former obviously and intensely so, and the latter because immanent in those processes are narratives, some of them human and some non-human. So what we eat, as much as the material food from which they are inseparable, are its *stories*. And those stories, being part of still bigger and older stories, never end. They are, in effect, inexhaustible.

In general, then, which stories would you like to take into yourself and become part of you? Ones in which healthy plants have been grown, tended, harvested and otherwise treated ethically, in ways that respect not only them but the biodiversity of which they are part and the soil whence they sprang, then prepared for a meal with skill and love? Or ones in which they have been treated like an already-dead thing, with no integrity of their own, industrially processed until almost nothing living remains, and sold for the highest possible price? To say nothing of fellow animals whose short, brutalised lives end in the death camps of industrial meat factories.

As I've said, in principle anything can enchant. Even a cheeseburger. But food that enchants truly is much more likely to have been grown and treated agroecologically – that is, organically, seasonally, and locally – and cooked skilfully in ways that have grown up in the area whence the plants themselves spring, thence in harmony with them. It's debatable ground, but there is also a case for eating animals, if one really must, who have been reared and killed or caught as painlessly as possible. (You see the problem, though?)

These rituals respect the integrity and autonomy of the food as the other party in a relationship. They don't, as per industrial agribusiness, simply impose human will on it, as if it were a dead object or a slave. Enchanting food will also almost certainly be eaten sitting down, not on the run; slowly, so its flavours can actually be tasted; and convivially, shared with others, whether friends or family. It will be slow food, not fast. If the food comes from far away, as my tangerines did, then one savours that too, and its exotic stories. (I won't belabour the resonances with sexual love – they are too obvious – except to say that in both, slowness is of the essence.)

Food, in all its metaphoric dimensions from physical to spiritual, nourishes communities and traditions as much as bodies. To pick only one example of many, in Florence locally sourced food creatively cooked in regionally traditional ways has, thanks to chef Fabi Picchi, provided the basis of the Cibrèo Città restaurant, café, trattoria, theatre/music-hall and club, along with all the convivial relationships which sustain and are sustained by them.

Nor is this sort of thing confined to the overdeveloped world. In the late 1990s, the Slow Food movement graduated to the developing world, where rich local knowledge of biodiversity and farming is under huge pressure from agro-industry. Terra Madre, its biennial showcase event, hosts cooks, artisans and farmers from all the world.

Moments

Of people who have based their lives and careers on the enchantment of food, few have written about it as well as M.F.K. Fisher. Here is a fragment of her account of encountering caviar for the first time, alternating with iced grassy vodka, aged twenty-three, in the Café de la Paix with her parents, as part of what she calls a 'luminous whole':

> We ate three portions apiece, tacitly knowing that it
> could never happen again that anything would be quite
> so mysteriously perfect... The headwaiter sensed all this,
> which is, of course, why he was world-known, and the

portions got larger, and at our third blissful command he
simply put the tin in its ice bowl upon the table… It was
reward enough to sit in the almost empty room, chaste
rococo in the slanting June sunlight, with the generous
tub of pure delight between us, Mother purring there,
the vodka seeping slyly through our veins, and real wood
strawberries to come, to make us feel like children again
and not near-gods.

And here is Elizabeth Bowen in Rome, eating a 'great ripe
Sicilian blood orange':

the peel, mottled satin outside, white velvet in, curls
away under digs from the thumbs, gladly; the delicate-
membraned sections fall asunder like petals, firm flesh
not spilling one drop of crimson juice until one bites into
them. Such oranges deserve to be eaten as I ate them, in
infiltrated sunshine, with wine to finish … Hour of vision
or hour of abeyance? Something of both go out with one
through the glass door.

I also warm to Stephen L. Kaplan, a professor from Brooklyn,
New York, who is consulted by about 1,000 artisanal French
bakeries a year. His culinary career began when he first tasted a
baguette in the Jardin du Luxembourg. 'The taste was bewitching.
I experienced a kind of vertigo of emotion and feeling. It was
Proustian experience with a Richter scale measure of 10.' Bread, says
Kaplan, should involve not only taste and smell but appearance,
texture, and the sound when it is broken or squeezed. A truly
excellent baguette, he says, can induce 'a great joy'.
    Is there something slightly ridiculous about the professor,
busily keeping Parisian *boulangers* up to the mark? I don't think so.
Upholding the potential wonder of food, even for the saps in the
McDonalds on Boulevard St Michel (and not all of them with the
excuse of being poor), is a worthy cause.
    While every part of the world has at least some local culinary

traditions, in certain national or regional cultures, enchanting food has an honoured place. Two of the foremost are France and Italy, where agroecology is flourishing, local and regional traditions and recipes abound, and meals largely remain highly social occasions. By the same token, in all three respects, there is determined (if uneven) resistance to American-style corporate fast food. The admirable Slow Food movement encourages and articulates that resistance, but it didn't create it.

When it comes to food, Anglo-American cultures are not enchantment-friendly. As the philosopher Michel Serres asks, 'When you condemn those who live to eat, you who speak of eating to live, have you worked out why you are living?' Even those who care are usually trying to make rational decisions based on the food's nutritional value, or else refusing to. In either case, disenchantment reigns. Meanwhile, colossal food-and-non-food conglomerates overwhelm supermarket shelves with 'edible food-like substances', in Michael Pollan's fine phrase, designed by 'food engineers', in the ghastly jargon of the industry, for 'eatertainment', 'craveability' and 'hedonics'. If any enchantment results from this sorcery, it is false: the desire to possess or be possessed.

When quantity entirely replaces quality, obesity and malnutrition follow, often among the same people. In the same way, alcohol judged solely by its strength encourages, and is encouraged by, disenchanted consumption: drinking in order to get drunk. Most alcoholic drinks have traditions of how they are made, against which one can judge whether they have been well or badly made, and appreciated or rejected. The breathless descriptions one finds nowadays, although absurd, are also oddly innocent. A beer is 'intensely hoppy, with a balance of subtle sweetness and velvety bitterness wrapped in a gloriously crispy body'. A cider is 'well-balanced between acidity and sweetness, with a long elegant end'. (I knew someone like that once.)

Pride of place, however, must surely go to wine, which probably offers an unmatched range of worlds of liquid enchantment. As Patrick Leigh Fermor observes, recalling a wine cellar near where the Moselle joins the Rhine, simply by sipping one could explore the two great rivers below and the Danube and all Swabia, and Franconia too by proxy… journeying in time from year to year, with draughts as cool as a deep well, limpidly varying from dark gold to pale silver and smelling of glades and meadows and flowers.

In fact, condensed into a single glass of wine is a concentrated essence of stories, natural and cultural, and times of all kinds in a moment, that would take a long book or more to relate one by one. No wonder Tolkien described finding the Finnish language for the first time as 'like discovering a complete wine cellar filled with bottles of an amazing wine of a kind and flavour never tasted before. It quite intoxicated me'.

Contrast such a wine with the industrial kind, made with formulas by corporate biochemists, adulterated with chemical agents and preservatives. It is blended, so it's from nowhere in particular and therefore has no stories to tell, and sold in vast quantities, crude, and cheap (although excellent local wines can be cheap too).

I'm not a wine-drinker, as it happens, but even I was once struck dumb by the taste of a *Monbazillac Jour de Fruit Domaine de l'Ancienne Cure* (the very name is poetry) when offered a glass by the woman with whom I was dining. The menu described it as 'Deep gold, honeyed, fat with peachy botrytis tones, gingerbread, hazelnuts, fresh mint and eucalyptus on the palate'. Gold is Aphrodite's colour, honey her sweetening, and peaches her fruit. Even now that I can, need I say more?

7. Learning

Niccolò Machiavelli has been exiled from Florence to his family farm. In a letter of 10 December 1513 to his friend Francesco Vettori, he wrote:

> On the coming of evening, I return to my house and enter my study... and reclothed appropriately, I enter the ancient courts of men of antiquity where, affectionately received, I partake of that food which alone is mine and for which I was born, where I am not too timid to speak with them and ask them the reasons for their actions; and they in their courtesy answer me; and for four hours of time I feel no weariness, I forget every trouble, I do not fear poverty, death does not dismay me; I give myself over entirely to them.

Three centuries later, John Ruskin praised the same 'aristocracy of companionship' with both the living and the dead that reading enables, requiring only 'a true desire to be taught by them, and to enter into their thoughts'. This court, he adds, 'is open to labour and to merit, but to nothing else. No wealth will bribe, no name overawe, no artifice deceive the guardian'.

The enchantment of learning has the same prerequisites and dynamics as other kinds, but we can think about it here in a way we haven't so far, namely through its affinity with play. This is no childish thing. Indeed, true maturity, Nietzsche suggests, requires 'rediscovering the seriousness one had as a child at play'. Play is present in any activities that are improvised (but not random), intentional (but not goal-directed), and metaphoric: doing or being as if one was also someone or something else.

It follows that where goals are preset and conclusions already known, for purposes other than knowledge itself for its intrinsic value – a better career, more money, respect of peers or any other use-value, no matter how defensible – highly structured learning shuts the door on enchantment. That requires a relationship between scholar or student (and every good scholar is also still a student) and subject in which the former may be personally affected by the latter, and wants above all to understand and appreciate it for its own sake. Only then can teaching open doors to the subject's wonder instead of it merely advancing preset goals or providing fodder for the lecturer or author. As Auden says, 'The primary requirement of a teacher – an interest in his pupils and a knowledge of educational techniques is secondary – is that he should be enchanted by the subject he teaches'.

Auden experienced this himself in Oxford in the 1920s as an undergraduate student of Tolkien. Tolkien was not particularly interested in his pupils and his educational technique was appalling, but his love of Old English, *Beowulf* and 'Northness' kindled a flame for Auden, among many others, that burned lifelong.

It's no secret that learning in the overdeveloped world, from schools for the very young all the way through to postgraduate study in universities, has been taken over by a government-backed business model that in its consumerism and instrumentalism – an obsessive emphasis on results, and on usefulness for career, status and salary – is the antithesis of enchantment.

Technodolatry works to the same end. Standardised impersonal technologies – keyboards instead of handwriting, computers instead of books – are pushed despite the fact that we know they result in poorer learning, retention and comprehension. MOOC's (Massive Open Online Courses) may be fine for disseminating information, but they eliminate the concrete magic of creative, improvisational interactions between teacher and student in a particular place and moment of actual, not virtual, reality. The amount of time that college students spend with professors, face-to-face – what do you know? – turns out to be the best predictor of their academic success.

That was my experience when I was lucky enough (blessed, I could as well say, or fated) to study under Gregory Bateson, in Santa Cruz, California, just before he retired. More than the anthropology or epistemology that provided the ostensible material, what happened was that in his presence, I learned to learn; or, I could say, to think. Not *how* to do it, note – students kept asking, in vain, for a method – but simply learning, by example, what it is *like* to learn or really think. Ludwig Wittgenstein asks, can one learn good judgment? He answers himself, 'Yes; some can. Not, however, by taking a course in it, but through "experience"... What one acquires here is not a technique; one learns correct judgments'.

Ruskin lamented of his Victorian contemporaries that 'It never seems to occur to the parents that there may be an education which, in itself, *is* advancement in Life;- that any other than that may perhaps be advancement in Death...' Collectively, we are now no better off and maybe worse. The Victorians never devised our ghastly metaphors, dead on arrival, which signal the disenchanted rule of modern capital: a knowledge economy, targets and outcomes, league tables, productivity, quantified impact assessments, transferable skills, human resources, core competencies or impact agendas.

This doesn't mean the enchantment of learning is extinct, of course. First of all, it flourishes in individuals when no one is looking. Amid the frantic feeding frenzies of social media, like countless minnows splashing in the shallows, here and there are readers diving deep into other minds.

To vary the metaphor slightly, writing is frozen thinking, but when it is read, felt and understood it melts and flows again, taking the mind of the reader with it. And what wonder, to find oneself connecting and communing with a great mind across an abyss of time, space and difference – technically long dead but come to life again in one's own mind, here and now! It is incredible to me that we could ever take this gift for granted.

Montaigne, for example, has had this effect on countless readers. For Stefan Zweig, 'Four centuries have gone up in smoke: it is not the Seigneur de Montaigne who is speaking to me... nor even a writer, but a friend who has come, to counsel and disclose himself'. Cyril Connolly, writing in 1944, on encountering the words of Sainte-Beuve, who lived in the first half of the nineteenth century, experienced 'Intense emotion, a mixture of relief and despair, at reading Sainte-Beuve's notebook *Mes Poisons*, and discovering "This is me".' This is a classic instance of finding oneself in a story, doubled, for me sixty years later, in the afternoon of 15 August 2011 in unlovely King Street, Hammersmith, when I read Connolly's words and with the same emotion found myself in them.

Enchantment survives in some colleges and universities, just as inspired teaching does in some schools, but despite them, not because of them. As the market and managerial model tightens its grip still further on institutions of learning, turning students, and potential citizens, into clients and customers, real learning and teaching is increasingly driven out and must go elsewhere. Now it is mostly found on the margins of the academy, in not-for-profit independent publications and websites, book clubs and informal discussion groups.

The model J.M. Coetzee describes, which came into being in Communist-ruled Central Europe, is being recalled under ruthless capitalism: 'the real university may have to move into people's homes and grant degrees for which the sole backing will be the names of the scholars who sign the certificates'.

The humanities – English literature, literary criticism and languages, the classics, history, the study of religion, art history and criticism, and those parts of anthropology and philosophy which haven't been annexed by science – hold powerful potential to enchant. They are far from perfect, of course, being beset by unexamined physics envy, an ingrained tendency to reduce everything to motives of 'identity' (gender, class or race), and a self-absorbed scholasticism.

Despite all that, metaphor remains the lifeblood of the humanities. There can be no understanding or interpreting the meaning of a person, action or idea without an empathic, imaginative or narrative understanding of them as someone or something else, an 'other' to the scholar, and what it means, what it is like, to be that other. And there is no pay off other than new, better or deeper understanding. The wonder when that happens is a sign telling us to listen up and pay attention.

Not surprisingly, therefore, the humanities are being starved in favour of STEM studies (science, technology, engineering and maths). They try to survive by appointing academics who are really managers in career drag and replacing the precious tradition of scholarly inquiry, which is obliged to wrestle with tensive truth, with the digital values of the new gods of disenchantment: neurophysiology, evolutionary biology and cognitive science. It is a pathetic sight. In a phrase that applies to all the humanities, Milan Kundera defines the wisdom of the novel as precisely 'the wisdom of uncertainty', as against the rule of either-or.

Don't mistake me. In certain situations, respecting the standard rules of logic is the right thing to do. Walt Whitman's flippant dismissal – 'Do I contradict myself? Very well then I contradict myself. (I am large, I contain multitudes)' – is only just saved from being exasperatingly irresponsible by being in a poem. In a discussion, it would bring any genuine exchange crashing to a close. But we don't need to treat those rules as infallible and sacrosanct, or appropriate in all situations. When one encounters genuine paradox, they should be allowed to give way. In the words of the great physicist Niels Bohr, 'The opposite of a fact is falsehood, but the opposite of one profound truth may very well be another profound truth'.

Wonder in learning, like the love it resembles, takes place only by personal involvement in example. It does not result from following a method, or depend on a method – let alone methodology, terminating in methodolatry, which has so completely seduced the modern academy. It cannot be applied, evaluated, improved or captured in an algorithm. Nor is it politically correct, although it is also not necessarily politically incorrect either; it is simply correctness-blind.

In this field too, enchantment is neither modern nor anti-modern but non-modern – which is to say, wild – and as such, it cannot survive being turned into a programme of any kind, including one of re-enchantment. As sometimes even its friends fail to realise, the most we can do to protect or promote enchantment in learning is to put our heart, mind and body into creating propitious conditions for it and then let it work its wonders, if it will.

8. Nature

One of the highlights of my life will always be hurtling along, crouched on the back of a sledge with my daughter sitting in front, pulled by a team of huskies through the northern Finnish forest, the sun glinting off snow crystals as we fly over frozen streams and thread through groves of solemn conifers. Exhilarating? Sheer aliveness. (No animals were harmed, by the way; these dogs love to run. The problem is getting them to stop!)

The natural world of your early years really gets under your skin. The spell it casts lasts, so at some very basic level you absorb the seasonal cycle, the angle of the light and the plants and the animals you first encounter, and they remain lifelong benchmarks. I have lived in England for more than four times as long as my youth in Canada, and I love the birds here, but even the most common-or-garden varieties – blackbirds, robins and blue tits, say – still look and feel slightly exotic.

My experience could be multiplied many times and ways. For this short account, I'll pick only one more. A Norwegian poet, Hans Børli, has praised the scent, 'sweet and naked', of freshly cut wood: 'as if life itself had walked by you, with dew in its hair'. It will, he says, be 'among the last things that you will forget'.

Nature has a double importance for us here. One is the many and rich experiences of enchantment in, and as, the natural world and its countless avatars. Its sweet benediction shines through even the deeply ingrained New England laconism of this report, for example, by a Mr E.O. Grant on 23 March 1926:

Saw farmer near Patten, Maine, sitting on a snowdrift about fifteen feet high, surrounded by a hundred redpolls.

Birds perched on the farmer's head and shoulders. One sat on knee. Farmer told [me] that he had enjoyed the previous half hour more than any other period in his life.

Such experiences are at once quietly common and mostly overlooked. They are even suppressed, sometimes for surprisingly misguided reasons. George Orwell asks,

> …is it politically reprehensible, while we are all groaning, or at any rate ought to be groaning, under the shackles of the capitalist system, to point out that life is frequently worth living because of a blackbird's song, a yellow elm tree in October, or some other natural phenomenon which does not cost money and does not have what the editors of left-wing newspapers call a class angle? There is no doubt that many people think so.

Thus Raymond Aron and his wife were once strolling in the Jardin du Luxembourg on a beautiful spring morning when they encountered Simone Weil in a flood of tears. When they asked her what was wrong, she replied, 'Do you mean you haven't heard? The Shanghai police have opened fire on the workers!'

I am not impugning Weil's moral integrity, nor political engagement. Nonetheless, I believe the modern Megamachine would prefer you were obsessed with current events on the other side of the world – which it will happily supply with 24-hour newsfeeds – than simply enjoying the natural world here and now, doing its own thing (not ours: disgraceful!). And this is not an issue of left vs right. As Orwell adds, 'spring is here, even in London N.1, and they can't stop you enjoying it', because 'the Earth is still going around the sun, and neither the dictators nor the bureaucrats, deeply as they disapprove of the process, are able to prevent it'.

The other kind of importance flows from the fact that ultimately, all experiences of enchantment are natural. From the most obviously 'physical' (sex, say, or food) to the most 'spiritual' (religion) and 'intellectual' (learning), all are instances of concrete magic realised by, and as, embodied beings. The very word 'human', from the Latin *humanus,* derives originally from the Indo-European *dhghem*, meaning 'earth', which also gives us 'humus'. It reminds us that we are Earthlings.

That is why it is dangerous nonsense to dream of 'conquering nature'. Victory in such a war would amount not only to ecocide – the murderous extermination of most non-human life on Earth – but collective suicide. It follows that the only sane definition of civilisation is the graceful accommodation and, when possible, celebration, of nature. Such a way of life wouldn't itself amount to enchantment, but it would leave plenty of room for it.

A word on the word 'nature'. What it means here is the more-than-human natural world that includes but vastly exceeds us, one species among millions. And it is alive, altogether as well as its parts. Those which are biologically alive engage in a complex dance with air, water, rock and soil, so that the Earth as a whole, including its abiotic parts, may live. Furthermore, everything that lives is particular, not generic or universal. As Merleau-Ponty elegantly puts it, there is 'a style of being wherever there is a fragment of being'. Thus it has, or rather is, a personality. Or in the words of Louis MacNeice (whose poetry often concerns enchantment): 'the only invulnerable Universal is one that is incarnate'.

Nature is also alive in the sense that it can come alive for us, regardless of its biological status. Of all the possible encounters and subsequent relationships, those with other animals probably result in the most common natural enchantment: wonder at this other being, its sheer presence. The resonance with 'love at first sight' is all to the point. Thus, for example, Horatio Clare remembers being 'bewitched' by 'a big and utterly beautiful red grouse'. 'That grouse,' he adds, 'made the morning surround him'.

Such enchantment further strengthens when one looks in the other's eyes and sees, and at the same moment is seen as, another person, with all that that entails: subjectivity, sentience and the capacity for suffering and joy. (There are many accounts of this happening with whales and dolphins, for example.) The other being non-human, and the gap between them and oneself being that much wider, the experience of meeting across it is all the more powerful.

So are the relationships with other animals growing from that seed, bearing a kinship which is durable and fundamental, in which enchantment is an inherent possibility. In a wonderful little essay about her friendship with a tiny lizard, Freya Stark says that 'I was filled with a constant wonder that a creature so small and so different, whose very blood was warmed by other laws than ours, should yet share these basic things – affection, trust, and an incredible perseverance and courage'. People who have experienced this sort of thing know that the other party, no matter if furry, feathered or scaly, is a non-human *person*, and they need no correcting by pompous scientistic authorities.

But such moments can be refused, never to return, in an impulse of human self-assertion which, upon examination, turns out to be based on fear and insecurity. D.H. Lawrence's poem 'Snake' is a peerless account of such a reaction, leaving him with a great sadness and 'something to expiate:/ A pettiness'. This too, I'm afraid, is human.

Another writer, Richard Mabey, also recounts an intense encounter with a bird, in this case a nightingale, one night in early May in the Suffolk countryside. He listens, rooted to the spot, and at that moment a shooting star flies overhead. As the unstoppable flow of notes 'fill the air' they seem 'to be doing odd things to the light', and 'just for a few seconds, the bird was in my head and it was me that was singing'. This is a classic instance of enchantment. All the important dynamics are at work: presence, concrete magic, the realisation of imagined wonder, impossible perfection and metaphor (Mabey is and is not the nightingale).

Neo-Darwinian disenchantment should not be allowed to take over here. In their complexity, subtlety and redundancy, the songs of the nightingale, blackbird, thrush and others far exceed what merely advertising territory and sexual fitness would require, even after granting that its full stretch. The best birdsong sounds unmistakably improvised within the relevant constraints of the organism, community and ecology – in other words, it is cultural

– while the best human improvisers sound unmistakably natural. (Sonny Rollins springs to mind.)

On rare occasions, natural enchantment is so powerful that it takes in the sort of divinatory personal address that occurred in the story of the balloon, earlier. It often centres on an animal, and certain kinds of animal clearly have a particular power to enchant us. (There is no reason to think enchantment is evenly or 'fairly' distributed in nature any more than elsewhere.) These include bears, foxes, wolves, lions, tigers, reindeer, whales and dolphins, owls, kingfishers, water-dippers, nightingales, swans, storks, ravens, turtles, salmon, honey bees and butterflies. And the animal who enchants is indissolubly both biological ('concrete' to the senses) *and* mythological ('magic' to the imagination), so any attempt to replace the latter with the former – that is, to completely naturalise it – destroys its enchantment.

Val Plumwood was an ecofeminist philosopher who championed wild nature all her life. On 30 March 2008, a few days after her death, she was buried on the mountain in Eastern Australia from which she had taken her surname. As friends shared memories and tributes around the cardboard coffin in which her body was lying, a large butterfly joined them, alighting on one person after another. Then, as there was a lull and some uncertainty about what should happen next, the butterfly landed on the deep pink flower that had been placed over Val's heart before suddenly flying straight up into the azure sky. By common consent, that was the signal to secure the lid and lower the coffin into the ground. I don't know how many of those present knew that the Greek word for the soul, *psūchê*, anglicised as 'psyche', also refers to a butterfly, but everyone there understood its truth at that moment.

Place

Places too can cast a spell. It is not surprising. After all, natural places, with some degree of ecosystemic integrity, share with animals intelligence (perceiving and reacting to their environment), emotions (giving rise to certain feelings) and intentionality (to persist and flourish). Presence, and perhaps relationship, is therefore perfectly possible.

Thus a young J.P. Donleavy, on a stop over between flights, walked out 'in the intoxicating clean, cool, moist fresh air' into the countryside, following a winding lane 'between iridescent velvet green pastures. To where I suddenly came upon a pond with three swans. In the lonely silence, their stunning eloquent whiteness on the gentle black water was miraculous…' This fateful encounter with 'Ireland in one of her graces' sealed where he would live for the rest of his life.

Fundamentally, whether or not a place is wild and to what degree, the fact is that we can only live in and through places. The range from rich and deep places to thin and impoverished is wide, but all places are particular. Even airports, shopping malls and motorways, if only just. Therefore places are also sensuous, qualitative and unique, each with its own personality which becomes unmistakable when they enchant us. Because places are, in their own way, personalities – even in cities, where they have been made over by us – they always can.

Henry Miller recalls a moment when he was riding the elevated line in Brooklyn, New York. Suddenly, Broadway, which he normally hated, changed. 'It wasn't that it became ideal or beautiful or unreal; on the contrary, it became terribly real, terribly vivid. But it had acquired a new orientation; it was situated in the heart of the world, and this world which I now seemed able to take in with one grasp had meaning… it simply belonged'.

This resonates with Tolkien's definition of *Faërie* as any place that contains us and the world when we, and it, are enchanted. But another, related understanding is also possible. Robert Bringhurst describes *Faërie* as 'the world beyond the daylight and the road, beyond the furrow and the fence, outside the reach of parliaments and church bells, where human institutions are not in control'. 'In North America,' he adds, 'we call this world Nature or the Wild', but it is equally 'the mythworld'.

Myth in this sense is the set of more-than-human meanings

which inhere in nature. Sean Kane's description of the proper subject of myth as 'the ideas and emotions of the Earth' confirms the point. Doesn't the Earth include even places like Broadway? And where exactly are human institutions really ever in control? Sometimes and to some extent, for sure, but never completely or for long. Wildness, unlike wilderness, can never be entirely kept out.

The true contrast with place is the notion of space. Universal, abstract, quantitative and uniform, space is disenchanted place. (Quantum and post-quantum weirdness has failed to dislodge Newtonian space in our practices, lives and minds.) We cannot live there – it is place, but on life-support – so the opposition is not quite symmetrical, but it can be used to support certain disenchanted programmes.

The ancient Greeks, who had a word for everything, were aware of the difference. They called space *topos*, while place was termed *chora*. The same contrast obtains between *Kairos*, a unique moment, and *chronos* or time, its universal and abstract ghost. Like place, moment can enchant, while time and space reduce that chance to almost nil.

Just as wildness can survive in cities, however, wilderness can sometimes be disenchanted. A few years ago, I was driving north in mid-Western Canada, to Lake Manitoba. I drove for an endless two hours through a disturbingly unchanging landscape of three colours – scrubby yellow-brown for the land, blue and grey for the sky – and two straight lines: the highway, disappearing up ahead, and the horizon. I felt increasingly agitated, until I finally exclaimed aloud, 'My god, there's nothing here!' Whereupon an inner voice glumly agreed: 'Yeah, man. It's *le néant*'. Later, I remembered that at about fourteen, in Winnipeg, I had read Sartre's *Nausea* and felt understood.

My experience then was not of the fecund Daoist void, nor the Buddhist emptiness of interdependency; it was the devouring maw of nothingness, with no way into it and no way out. Without an engaged imagination (something we shall explore later), the vastest wilderness is a prison, whereas enchantment, in the words of John

Donne, 'makes one little room an everywhere'. The same is true of an eternity of endless linear time, as against a single inexhaustible moment.

Pursuing the Greek connection further, moment and place together make up *mythos*, while space and time are *logos*, its overweening child who claims sovereignty. But *logos* – Word, theory, system – is itself inescapably mythic and specifically Apollonian, while the boast to have conquered myth is that of the vainglorious male Hero. So too is the claim to have replaced myth, now classed as ignorant lies and delusions, with science. That is why, as the modern mystic John Moriarty writes, 'myth not maths is the mother tongue'. Even the denial of myth takes place on mythic ground.

In earlier chapters we thought through enchantment with the help of Aphrodite, especially as love, and Hermes, especially as art. So what is the mythic provenance of nature? It is the Earth itself – or rather, since the impersonal pronoun is singularly unsuitable here, and the Earth is the source of life – herself, and when she reveals herself in a moment of enchantment it is (to borrow an excellent word from the writer Tim Robinson) a geophany: a showing forth of the Earth.

Much has been written by others about Gaia, so I will approach the subject from a slightly different angle. William James, a philosopher whose work is highly sympathetic to enchantment, quotes this account by a now obscure German writer, Gustav Theodor Fechner. While Fechner was out walking one spring morning,

> a light as of transfiguration lay on all things. It was only
> a little bit of the Earth; it was only one moment in her
> existence; and yet as my look embraced her more and more
> it seemed to me not only so beautiful and ideal but so true
> and clear a fact, that she is an angel, an angel so rich and
> fresh and flower-like, and yet going her round in the skies
> so firmly and so at one with herself, turning her whole
> living face to Heaven, and carrying me along with her into

that Heaven, that I asked myself how the opinions of men could ever have spun themselves away from life so far as to deem the Earth only a dry clod, and to seek for angels above it or about it in the emptiness of the sky – only to find them not…

James concurs, 'Yes! The Earth is our great common guardian angel, who watches over all our interests combined'. And he asks, after Fechner, what good can come of a doctrine that any God must be transcendent, bodiless and bloodless, while nature is rendered soulless and meaningless, an exercise in mechanics in which life itself becomes an anomaly?

This splitting of concrete magic is the foundational act of disenchantment. Its 'primitive unity', as Weber calls it, is divided into either material or spiritual – 'rational cognition and mastery of nature, on the one hand, and into "mystic" experiences, on the other'. Its principal metaphysical root is, of course, Platonism, in which the so-called material world comprises mere shadows, copies, reflecting the spiritual world of pure Ideas. But modern materialism merely inverts the dualism it inherited by hypervaluing the former instead, leaving whatever cannot be measured, managed and mastered as (in Weber's words) 'the only possible "beyond," added to the mechanism of a world robbed of gods'.

Each side is then apportioned to experts, both official and unlicensed: scientific on the one hand and theological on the other. Nothing is allowed to not be one or the other, or both. Ambiguity, gaps and any third thing are intolerable, because then total mastery through calculation becomes impossible. In the process, enchantment is driven out. The price is meaninglessness, resulting in and encouraging nihilism. Young people in particular are starved of values that aren't instrumental and ultimately mercenary.

Recalling the point that enchantment is love for things whether 'animate' or 'inanimate', we can even respond to the Earth's primary abiotic constituents, anciently symbolised by the symbolic elements of fire, earth, air and water. The nineteenth-century writer Richard Jefferies records being enchanted by the firmness of the

Earth, bearing him up; the purity of the air (not being in London at the time); the sea's strength; and the sun, 'his light and brilliance'. But included in these were their soul equivalents. While drinking water, for example, 'clear as light itself in solution, I absorbed the beauty and purity of it'.

Indeed, you can be enchanted by something as apparently abstract as Northness, for example. But then it becomes a whole bodymind experience. When J.B. Priestley found himself in northern British Columbia, quite unexpectedly his soul 'sent up a shout of delight'. Another writer, Cynthia Ozick, a denizen of New York City, was in Jutland one November afternoon when 'enchantment swept me through and through. It was very nearly a kind of seizure: an electrifying pang that shook me to tears of recognition... it came to me all at once that north was where I had once belonged, north was the uncanny germ of my being'. A third, Russell Hoban, finds North-in-itself looking at him from the luminous golden eyes of a snowy owl. 'You're far away, I say. I'll never go to the north. Everything has its north, says the north. I'll come to you'.

Places which enchant are often liminal or riparian, as edges and boundaries – debatable ground between the sea and the land, say, or between wilderness and domestication. Conversely, where uniformity and homogeneity reign, so does disenchantment.

By the same token, transitional and therefore ambiguous times of the day and of the year are potentially the most enchanting: dawn (between first light and sunrise) and dusk (between sunset and darkness), and seasonally, autumn and spring. At noon and in high summer, enchantment is dazzled and dispersed; at midnight and in mid-winter, it sleeps deep. As Karen Blixen, an unfailing guide to enchantment, says:

> day is a space of time without meaning... it is with the coming of dusk, with the lighting of the first star and the first candle, that things will become what they really are, and will come forth to meet me.

Naturally, when the diurnal and annual coincide, enchantment and disenchantment are potentially doubled: the former at twilight in autumn, say, and so on.

Certain other natural phenomena also tend to enchant. These include, for example, the Northern Lights, rainbows, and autumn foliage. Surely anyone who has encountered these at their best has been left in wonder. But such wondering slides, unless one is wary, into a different kind that then attracts responses which tend to disenchant. This largely results from a confusion (and not always by honest error) between the question 'How?' and the question 'Why?'

Earlier, I said that enchantment obviates the need for any questions. But children, as we know, are epic questioners, so they will often turn to the first and most fundamental question of all: why? And when the child asks, 'Why do the leaves turn red and yellow?', they may be answered, 'Well, because the Earth is revolving around the Sun at an angle, the light now is getting less, and that causes certain chemicals to be produced in the leaves, which...' Or: 'The Northern Lights are a result of the way charged particles from the Earth's magnetic field behave at high altitudes...' Or: 'Rainbows are caused by the optical refraction of and reflection of water drops in the air...'

Why do these explanations disenchant? Because when they are taken to be exhaustive, they reduce what actually presents itself to something else supposedly more important and therefore more valuable and interesting – the ions, particles, chemicals and so on to which physics and chemistry lay claim – of which the phenomenon itself then becomes merely a generic effect. The explanation thus comes to replace, in the mind of the perceiver, the glowing sky itself, or the multicoloured rainbow arc, or the swirl of red, orange and yellow leaves. (This is reduction 'down'. There is also reduction 'up', to God.)

Such disenchantment depends on the false assumption that in answering 'How?' you have also answered 'Why?' But the latter is an entirely different order of question, and both it and its answers escape the causal net of scientific explanation, no matter how fine. Those answers, if genuine, are never universal or generic. They require a response unique to the inquirer in each particular case, to what is encountered. This was what Wittgenstein meant when he remarked, 'Our children learn in school already that water *consists* of the gases hydrogen and oxygen, or sugar of carbon, hydrogen and oxygen. Anyone who doesn't understand is stupid. The most important questions are concealed'. Questions of 'Why?' concern *meaning*, and as such, they can only be answered personally and in metaphor. As D.H. Lawrence noted, 'With our bodies we know that water is *not* H_2O, our intuitions and instincts both know it is not so. But they are bullied by the impudent mind'.

A friend reported his experience of a total eclipse of the Sun thus:

> There were gasps and shouts and exclamations at the extraordinary moment when the last sliver of the Sun disappeared, instantly replaced by a deep black circle surrounded by a corona of ghostly white light... Time was suspended until a reddish-yellow light burst out triumphantly on the other side of the dark circle and the corona instantly vanished. I felt like I had been present at an ancient, exalted ritual of the gods.

Trusting the mind's spontaneous choice of metaphor, and distrusting attempts to second-guess it in accord with current orthodoxy, I would only add: yes, you were, and how marvellous!

The disenchanters like to imagine they have escaped the ambit of metaphor and myth, which they identify with tradition, superstition and error. In modern societies, of course, they have largely had their way. When one great resister, William Blake, was asked 'when the Sun rises do you not see a round Disk of fire somewhat like a Guinea?', he replied 'O no no I see an Innumerable company of the Heavenly host crying Holy Holy Holy is the Lord God Almighty'. Why not? But the point is that these are equally metaphors, the disk of fire as much as the Heavenly host. No one is seeing the sun 'as it actually is', because the 'is' can never be cashed in except as another metaphor, a seeing-*as*, whether it's a flaming ball of gas or an angel.

Thus has arisen the modern belief that nature is 'actually' nothing but a blank canvas, an inert, featureless nothingness whose only meanings are whatever humans, consciously or unconsciously, 'project' onto it. All subjectivity and agency is thus reserved for the human mind alone, to deploy or not as it will. This absurd Cartesian fantasy, pandering as it does to human vanity, has penetrated the most sophisticated cultural and intellectual corners. What matters more, however, is its convenience for those operating the Earth-destroying machinery of corporation, committee room and laboratory. If there is nothing and no one else really out there, why does it matter what we do to it? Ethics become irrelevant, since no relationship, let alone partnership or solidarity, is supposedly possible.

Thus high theory, violently abstracting, conspires with low profit-motive to bring about the disenchantment of the world. Living nature and its myriad qualities are turned into mere quantitative stuff to be measured, carved up and sold off, which is justified by 'ecosystem services', 'natural capital' and other euphemisms for exploiting and enslaving. Meanwhile, not only the suffering and violent deaths of billions of animals for our delectation but the massacre of the few remaining wild animals continues apace.

Disenchantment is a fundamental prerequisite for the entire process. Only people with a fierce but nonpossessive love of the other – this park, field or forest, these trees here, those animals there – who have realised their intrinsic value, regardless of their use to us and market value, will fight to protect them. Disenchanted business-as-usual welcomes reason alone, because it is easily corrupted by selfish and short-term arguments.

As Blake observes, 'The tree which moves some to tears of joy is in the Eyes of others only a Green thing that stands in the way'. But, he adds, 'to the Eyes of the Man of Imagination, Nature is Imagination itself'. Potent stuff! I understand it to mean that in enchantment, we realise nature truly – that is, as concrete magic. Both material and spiritual, it is a fact that is also a story and a story that is also a fact. The more-than-human natural world is physical stuff all the way up and metaphoric meaning all the way down. There is no such thing as 'just stuff', any more than there is 'just story'.

For the same reason, enchantment also cannot survive being parsed as either 'inner' or 'outer', or any calculated combination of the two. Being radically nonmodern, let alone Cartesian, it is completely and inseparably both. In enchantment, what is the case generally becomes striking: 'The world is wholly inside, and I am wholly outside myself'. These words by Merleau-Ponty are no Gallic extravagance but an exact and parsimonious description.

Animism

There is a practice that keeps the door open to that kind of perception and apprehension and encourages them, making a healthy relationship with more-than-human nature possible. Even for city-dwellers! After all, there is no wilderness in a city but there is still wildness. The name for it is 'animism', meaning a disciplined habit of staying open to personhood, subjectivity and agency whenever, wherever and in whatever form one encounters it. That may be a squirrel, a crow, a tree, a stone, a building or, of course, another human.

This point returns us to religion, except that what we are talking about is more a sort of personal but ultimately collective spirituality. It has no need of God or supernatural beings (although it is not so dogmatic as to rule them out), because in the words of the Zen master Shunryu Suzuki, 'The world is its own magic'.

I believe an animist sensibility is the oldest and most natural, as well as sanest, kind of religion. It is our birthright as Earthlings, and even after centuries of training in disenchantment, philosophical, religious and latterly scientific, it only takes a moment of real enchantment to reawaken it, and us. We could also describe it as aboriginal, since it is our original condition, or indigenous, since that signifies a kind of relationship to place, the land and the Earth. (It decidedly does not refer, as per a recent unpleasant recrudescence of racism and eugenics, to a bloodline. Old lies sounds no better in new mouths.)

But we need reminders. These are often unexpected, taking us in directions against the general human flow. In an ever-increasingly crowded, noisy, over heated and brightly lit world, for example, it is often their less popular contraries that stand out and offer the solace of wonder. Without a measure of solitude, you don't know who you are – something which online and mediated life has grievously accelerated – and without boundaries, no meeting is possible. Take away quiet against which sound can stand out and register as distinct – the 'concrete' without which there is no 'magic' – and it becomes not only deafening but meaningless, mere noise. Ever higher temperatures mean we are losing to lassitude what Charles Dickens calls 'clear, bright, jovial, stirring cold; cold, piping for the blood to dance to'. (There are days in winter now that are so warm I can't go out with a coat on. It's just wrong.)

We also grossly overvalue light while irrationally fearing darkness, or Mother Night, as one professor I know calls her. And mother *of* the light. Identifying light with *logos*, reason, heaven and maleness drives us to disparage the sources of enchantment in *mythos*, emotion, Earth and the female. It is not so much the dreams of reason that produce monsters as sleepless reason. 'No one,' proclaimed the Enlightenment philosopher Fichte ominously, 'has any rights against reason'. Political terror, from Paris to Phnom Pen, has always invoked this assertion. Meanwhile, in the only form of universal illumination we have actually come close to attaining – rampant light pollution from the 24-hour economy – millions of birds are dying, either from flying, dazzled, into buildings, or slowly, from disrupted migratory patterns, while the stars of the night sky, one of the most ancient and potent sources of wonder, are steadily disappearing from urban view.

Natural Enchantments

All the more reason, then, to value wonder at nature when and where we still can. Let me continue in the vein of Northness, cold and darkness for a moment. The winter solstice, in the Northern hemisphere, is when the Sun finally stages its annual resurrection, and its light begins to increase once more. But I am not reducing Yule, Saturnalia, or the birth of Mithra and Jesus to an astronomical event subsequently interpreted to mean new life. Rather, as is always the case with enchantment, the factuality comes already imbued with metaphorical meaning. It is whole cloth; they appear together.

This is what allows the turn of the year to be celebrated as Christmas without forcing a religious reduction. A poem by R.S. Thomas, for example, is deeply informed by his Christianity but at the same time transcends it, celebrating the red on snow's white of 'the one/ Robin, that is like a fire/ To warm by and like Christ/ Comes to us in his weakness,/ But with a sharp song.' And Laurie Lee recalls carolling outside the farmhouses and mansions of his Gloucestershire valley in the freezing winter night, with its great halls, the stars to show kings their way, and the beasts stamping in their stalls, making two thousand Christmases real – a realisation of imagined wonder we, his readers, are lucky enough to share.

The poignancy of enchantment, its passingness, is strong in the natural enchantment of snow. Who hasn't been delighted by the beauty of a newly snow-covered world in the morning, replacing the grey blocks and spiky bareness of the night before? (I can almost hear someone say: the homeless, or those who still need to get to work. I don't deny suffering, great or little, of course. Only remember that there is no need to choose between them. Or would you deny even the possibility of wonder to those already in dire need?)

In England, the last proper Snow Day – schools and businesses closed, roads impassable and trains stopped, play the only serious option – took place on 2 February 2009. Noisy, dirty, unfriendly London returned, in the words of a normally tough-minded

Guardian journalist, 'to a forgotten innocence… My God, I told myself as I walked through a heavenly avenue with snow-laden branches bejewelling my steps, this is the most beautiful city in the world!' Professionally ill at ease in *Faërie*, he concluded that he was 'in need of a good slap'.

Fluffy, wet snow on branches strongly suggests the blossoms that will follow. It is striking how strongly these most evanescent of natural phenomena can enchant. In part, at least, that very vulnerability is surely why. But I think a related reason is that blossoms, in shades of red-brown, pink and white, ineluctably suggest carnality. Metaphorically invoking our own transient flesh, their wonder reminds us, wordlessly, that passing cannot finally be separated from being here at all. (Those who try to avoid passing are therefore doomed to spend their lives not really living.)

In March 1994, three months before he died of pancreatic cancer, the playwright Dennis Potter told his interviewer that outside his study window, there was not just 'nice blossom' but 'the whitest, frothiest, blossomest blossom that there ever could be, and I can see it'. Need we wait so long, both individually and collectively, to see it for ourselves?

9. Disenchantment

Disenchantment needs its own chapter. Let's begin by distinguishing it from ordinary non-enchantment, a simple fact of normal daily life. It returns when enchantment passes, and enchantment only stands out, indeed, is only possible, against that background.

We can take this point further. Since we can visit but not stay in *Faërie*, sometimes it is necessary, for psychic survival – to prevent things tipping into addiction, say, or some related pathology – to say, 'Maybe that's enough now.' In the words of Thomas Mann, 'Not to be able to desire wholesome disenchantment is to be licentious.' But how to enact that?

In a tale collected by W.B. Yeats, one wild night Michael Hart finds himself in the power of two strange men who will not let him go until he tells them a story. After an initial refusal and its consequence (they 'put me out like a shot'), all he can think to relate is how he came to be there, in their power. 'That will do,' says one, and he wakes up free, the next morning, in a field. Perhaps simply telling a story, the very act of doing which honours the narrative heart of enchantment, offers a way out of its power without disrespecting or trying to destroy it.

By the same token, in another old story the King of Elfland says a charm 'which takes away every last bit of enchantment'. And in *Little, Big*, John Crowley's wondertale, an elemental spirit offers the helplessly sceptical Smoky an old Gladstone carpetbag which is extraordinarily capacious. It's even got pockets, he says, 'for your unbelief'. (Once on the Outside, the bag turns into an old wasp's nest, reminding us that enchantment's coin has no value back in the grey and leafless world. But that doesn't make the latter any more real than the former. Nor are the two worlds completely separate; some psychic analogue of the bag stays with Smoky long after he has forgotten the event.)

It seems to me that these stories hint at something else important, too. If enchantment is indeed our fundamental condition, then perhaps disenchantment is – or can be understood as, and thereby altered – enchantment of a peculiar mood and power. This point runs in tandem with another just mentioned, that when *logos* – rationalism, order, the word – claims victory over *mythos*, that is itself a mythic claim. Both ideas taken together make even more sense if the alternative is to accept the claims of the scientistic disenchanters to see things 'objectively', as they really are, from nowhere in particular. Now that really is unbelievable!

Regarding full-blown disenchantment – as a thing in itself, so to speak not merely a lack of enchantment – let's recall that true enchantment is wonder, for which the corresponding emotion is non-possessive love and the appropriate attitude is fearless receptivity. What then are its contraries? There are at least two. One is Apollonian order which manifests, for example, as bureaucratic management, often accompanied by an attitude of interference, inducing boredom. The other is Dionysian passion as cruelty, in particular, accompanied by the desire to inflict, and inducing, terror. (Cruelty, says Montaigne, is the worst thing we do.)

Both modes are forms of power-over, as against wonder-at. It follows that the most intense disenchantment results from their combination: the rational administration of fear. So the contrary of enchantment at its most radical – sheer kindness, selfless love – is routine torture. Thus, Jean Améry observed the 'serious, tense faces' of his S.S. torturers 'concentrated in murderous self-realisation. With heart and soul they went about their business, and the name of it was power, dominion over spirit and flesh…' In Cyril Connolly's bitter quip, 'Perfect fear casteth out love'.

When a death-camp guard dashed an icicle out of Primo Levi's mouth as he was trying to assuage his thirst and Levi asked, 'Why?', the reply – 'There is no why here' – voiced that terrible place as a perfect inversion of the overflowing meaning, sufficient unto itself and silencing all questions, of deep enchantment. But these are far from the only possible examples. Even allowing for historical specificity, as the philosopher Paul Feyerabend says, 'Auschwitz-Birkenau is an extreme manifestation of an attitude that still thrives in our midst'. And Nazism although egregious and in its way unique, is not the only manifestation. Stalin's Russia, Mao's China and Pol Pot's Cambodia, among others, were as terminally disenchanting, and anyone willing to overlook that fact (as far too many intellectuals have been and are) is complicit.

The same impulses and imperatives combine in another way. The programme of modernity is the rational pursuit of mastery, which is supposed to guarantee control and therefore security. No one has analysed modernity with more acute and bracing bleakness than Max Horkheimer and T.W. Adorno, and its ideal, they say, is 'the system from which everything and anything follows'. That in turn requires a single universal principle to enable all things to be calculated, compared and controlled. Its application to all situations, places and people is the rationalisation and bureaucratisation which results in the disenchantment of the world. The tyranny of a single metric, and the corresponding value, is its essence. Hence the fetish now made of algorithms.

Built into the model of the supposedly universal Truth is what Adorno calls 'the violence of unity'. We live in an inherently messy, unbounded, glorious and terrible world which we can only learn to see as unitary and uniform, and instruct others to. We can certainly give reasons, but as Wittgenstein asks, 'how far do they go? At the end of reasons comes *persuasion*. (Think what happens when missionaries convert natives.)'

The master principle only works if it is single, with no others on an equal footing, and universal, true everywhere without exceptions. Anything plural and incommensurable resists mastery by calculation, so it must be turned into what *can* be calculated. The standard procedure, as Horkheimer and Adorno say, is to make 'dissimilar things comparable by reducing them to abstract quantities', and anything left over is then treated as illusory.

Disenchantment is thus required and actively sought. It demands 'the extirpation of animism... All gods and qualities must be destroyed'. Why? Animism because a living nature is wild, not under our control; gods because each one embodies a unique principle, valid unto itself but limited by the others, without a single principle to rule them all; and qualities because unlike quantity, they are necessarily plural. (That is, the singularity of each depends on the others from which it differs.)

This world-historical exercise in the will-to-power has assumed unprecedented proportions in modern times, although its roots lie in monotheism. Traditionally, the single universal principle was supplied by God. Religious disenchantment continues in force, of course. But the modern secular version has replaced Him with Truth. From divinely instituted order to the motto of McKinsey, the global consultancy firm also known as 'the Brotherhood', has proved a surprisingly short step: 'Everything can be measured and what gets measured gets managed.' It's a lie, of course – in both parts – and very few actually believe it, any more than they still do (outside the Bible Belt) in the literal resurrection of the flesh on Judgement Day; but it has such power in our world that very many are obliged to pretend to believe it or, worse, act as if they did.

Scientific materialism and religious supernaturalism are thus the two great disenchanting monisms. That is why Horkheimer and Adorno say that 'Reason *and* religion deprecate and condemn the principle of magic enchantment'. Adherents of both compete for power. Secretly, however, they support each other by upholding the shared ideal of overall control and the shared mode of abstracting all concrete magic. (It also follows that anyone questioning this will be attacked from both directions.)

Having already discussed religious disenchantment, I shall concentrate here on the modern secular version. Its distinctiveness lies in having abandoned any remaining incalculability in principle, namely the mystery of an ultimately unknowable and unfathomable God, and absorbed the Mosaic imperative to always ask, 'Is this from or of the one true God, or not?' into the Platonic imperative to always ask, 'Is this true or not?' Hence Nietzsche's *cri de coeur* from the heart of our, not his, madness: 'The "apparent" world is the only one: the "true" world is merely *added by a lie*'.

That lie is repeatedly advanced by scientistic writers, falling over themselves to portray the universe as one of utter disenchantment: 'blind, pitiless indifference', in the words of one, while another describes human life as a 'farcical' accident in a 'hostile' universe which is 'pointless'. But it cannot be plausible asserted that our lives definitely or ultimately have no significance, including enchantment. Given how many imponderables the grand scheme of things entails, not only factually but in principle, we simply have no way of finally *knowing*. And to quote Mary Midgley (a philosopher who single-handedly shows us that as G.K. Chesterton always claimed, sanity can be enchanting) 'This cosmos is, after all, the one that has produced us and has given us everything that we have. In what sense, then, is it hostile? Why this drama?'

On the level of global governance, the effect of trying to be purely rational is that Apollonian administrative logic serves Dionysian desire-premises which it cannot acknowledge or analyse. The result, to quote Horkheimer and Adorno again, is that 'faith's irrationality' turns into 'rational organisation in the hands of the utterly enlightened, as they steer society toward barbarism'. Isn't that just where we are today?

Even calling this a 'programme' may be too much of a concession to disenchanting abstraction. I prefer a term from the historian of ideas Lewis Mumford: the Megamachine. This predatory monster – gleaming, smooth, seemingly all-powerful – has three engines that work together, to coin a phrase, in one ring of power. Let's consider each in turn.

Capital

The master motor is corporate capital. Having taken over God's universality while dropping His mystery, money has come to be the most perfect possible realisation of one truth, one system and one rule. Everything is fungible in the acid bath of exchange- and use-value. This is, as Robert Bly says, 'the sad little song hummed by Ph.D. candidates and politicians and experts in government planning: "One thing equals another thing."' It does if you make it; for a while, and up to a point. Admittedly, this is a little tough on Ph.D. candidates. The point is that such a mode is ruinous for wonder, since every activity and product is stripped of its unique value and reduced to a means to some other end.

Capital needs and seeks disenchantment because the concreteness and therefore potential enchantment of a person or forest or painting cannot by exchanged with a 'similar', 'comparable' or even 'indistinguishable' one. Its intrinsic value, which enchantment partly reveals and partly creates, makes it literally price-less. For capital, such resistance is unwelcome. What it seeks is a free flow of money, circulating unimpeded by any other values, and to that end it tries to commodify the whole of our lives, from cradle to grave, in one megamonopoly. That includes love, friendship, trust and respect, in the profitable ways it defines them – social media's *forte*.

One of the principal ways capital works is through glamour, a zombie simulacrum of enchantment which can be controlled and manipulated. It is the task of the marketing, advertising, public relations and political spin industries, with their multi-billion-pound budgets, to create and manage glamour. As Auden says, 'Propaganda, commercial or political, might be defined as the employment of magic by those who are not susceptible to its spells against those who are'.

Glamour in turn manufactures false enchantment: the desire to possess or be possessed. Since that desire cannot really satisfy the soul, it is insatiable, and consumers keep on coming back for more, which then repeats the cycle: corporate paydirt. (Even the desire for possession is a parody of true yearning, which the enchanted may well value more than any proposed gratification of it.)

Two of the largest and most powerful marketing and advertising companies in the world are Facebook and Google. They are not in business in order to connect you with your friends or help you find out information. That's just part of how they *do* business: by offering you 'free' services in order to harvest your data (I prefer the metaphor 'mine') and sell it on, extremely profitably. As Eric

Schmidt, currently executive chairman of Alphabet Inc., owners of Google and YouTube, puts it: 'We know where you are. We know where you've been. We can more or less know what you're thinking about'. (It sounds as if he was rehearsing for a part in *The Godfather*.)

Fetishising information has a huge side-benefit for the Megamachine: it is deeply disenchanting. Weber, if you remember, says that all that is required for the disenchantment of the world is the belief – when sufficiently widespread, supported and developed – 'that one can in principle, master all things by calculation'. And what is a search engine such as Google but that belief incarnate? We need to make a huge effort of will even to remember that it's nothing but a belief, or that there are many things, some of them extremely important, which cannot be mastered at all, let alone by calculation.

The bargain that results is the one figured by Goethe as Faust, the modern man who is willing sacrifice all relationships, values and principles – and if not, life itself – for the knowledge that promises mastery, security and ultimately immortality. But the temptation is old and runs deep. It was the seductive song of the Homeric Sirens, for what did they use to lure men to their death? The promise of ever more, total and perfect knowledge. Hence, as Auden says, 'The notion that something might be true but worthless or evil for us to know, that there could be anything we are capable of knowing but should refrain from discovering, has become inconceivable'.

The data which internet companies collect also acts as raw material for a related industry which happens to be one of two in which Google has massively invested: artificial intelligence. The other is robotics, in tandem with and increasingly indistinguishable from biotechnology, and their combination is now the holy grail of a fully managed and monetarised (which is to say, disenchanted) world.

All that is needed to complete the picture is entertainment for the masses, ever-increasingly unemployed or miserably employed, especially in the form of games consoles and virtual reality devices (also for sale, of course), to take your mind off the fact that that world itself has become so unfulfilling. Many people already alternate between Apollonian rationalised boredom – the day job/self – and compensatory Dionysian release – the night life/self – thus passing over enchantment, that subtle but vital third thing, in both directions. (I am constantly struck by large public ads for films that brag about them being terrifying, violent, horrific, etc. Surely no one, unless psychopathic, could find this a positive experience if grid-ruled tedium didn't loom large in their daily life.)

Modern life is full of disenchantments which fall short of directly life-threatening but can still induce a loss of the will to live: tax returns, job and grant applications, traffic queues, giant supermarkets and that form of low-level torture, budget and economy air-travel. Then there is the evil of banality whereby one is inescapably subjected, in public places, to terminally boring conversations on mobile phones. Just as enchantment means not for sale, privatisation is the quintessential act of disenchantment; it replaces the different selves of relationship, the prerequisite for enchantment, with a universal Me. In this case, the ubiquity of mobile phones amounts to a massive privatisation of a formerly public commons which has gone almost completely uncontested, so mesmerised are most people by 'convenience'.

For the ultimate symbol of modern madness, however, step forward the leaf blower. Replace a cheap, simple and reasonably effective rake or broom with a complex machine that runs on fossil fuel, pollutes the air and makes an insane amount of noise? Yes, as Robin Williams used to say, give me more of that! (There is competition, it's true, from those maddening motor-scooters that infest towns and cities at night: leaf-blowers on wheels.)

It's not difficult to feel the shiny new barbarism that is coming: a fully rationalised, modernised, capitalised society. Yet it is supported not only by those who would directly profit but by the much greater number of morally negotiable careerists upon which the administration of every empire has always depended. (When journalist Ellen Ullman voiced her concerns about a new app to assess potential employees' 'cultural fit', the man promoting it replied, 'Well, all that may be true, but I'm not working for society. I'm working for the company'.) And beyond them there is an army, nearly all men, spending far more time online and believing far too much of what they absorb there than is healthy, who are terrified of ending up on the wrong side in this crypto-eschatological narrative of winners and losers. Smart jackboots? Whatever it takes.

Even relatively innocent uses of the internet play their part in this disenchanting trajectory. They infantilise us, ramping up the narcissism of selfie-me and my demands and encouraging fantasies of 'freedom' from being an animal – embodied, socially embedded and utterly dependent on the ecology of the Earth, whose dynamics are not only literally vital but the wellsprings of enchantment. In this respect, the transhumanist ravings of Ray Kurzweil, Silicon Valley's own prophet, are only an extreme version of a frighteningly widespread attitude. And last time I checked, he was the head of engineering for Google.

Then there is the 'continuous partial attention' that results from being 'connected' 24/7. Almost everyone is distracted, almost all of the time. Enchantment rarely happens if you are not present for it, and the digital tsunami of information keeps us hooked while it devours ever greater chunks of our precious and limited attention.

At the same time, enchantment depends on there being gaps in your life when you are relatively autonomous and therefore open to the possibility of relationship. But connection is becoming a substitute for relationship, and hyper-connectedness means that the gaps are closing. Texts, emails, Instagram pages, Twitter feeds, news, phone calls, videos, Tinder, WhatsApp, Facebook pages – to never be 'out of touch', to never be alone with yourself, to be managed 24/7, by yourself when not by bosses, colleagues, friends or parents, kills off one of its essential preconditions. And as enchantment drains away, so does deep meaning: intrinsic values, ultimate values, values which are not for sale. Is it surprising, then, that depression and suicide rates among young people have surged since 2010? The only significant change since then is a corresponding rise in social media use.

There are now a few signs of resistance, not to mention almost comical desperation: mindfulness apps, apps to help you not use your phone so much, apps to limit the number of apps you use. (OK, I made the last one up. But how long before it's true?) It is also now common knowledge that great effort and ingenuity has gone into designing social media for addiction, the undermining of impulse control and continuous attention-grabbing, exploiting developmental and emotional vulnerabilities and susceptibility to peer-group pressure. But with former executives and engineers of Facebook, Google and Apple lining up to warn of the dangers of the monster they helped create, I don't need to belabour the point. We should have listened to Steve Jobs's response back in 2010 to a question about how his children liked the new iPad: 'They haven't used it. We limit how much technology our kids use at home'.

When they were both living in Palo Alto in the later 1970s, Jobs presented my Zen teacher, Kobun, with a prototype Apple personal computer as proof that he, Jobs, was enlightened. Kobun later commented wryly that he thought Jobs's children were better proof. (Whether or not they themselves would agree is another matter.)

There is another aspect of these developments with particular relevance to enchantment. Code, the bloodless heart of computerisation, digitalisation and algorithms, is binary: either a 0 or a 1. In the world of code/space there is no in-between, no ambiguity, and no gap that may be crossed by an encounter from which something new could spring, so enchantment becomes homeless. Indeed, nothing alive is any version of an exhaustive either/or. By implication, a sufficiently empowered code doesn't need, or maybe want, us. After all, the perfect system would run itself, free from the stupid errors and tiresome qualms of human operators.

This is no mere fantasy. Don't underestimate the extent to which fundamental aspects of modern societies are already determined by algorithms, not understood even by their inventors, and completely unaccountable: 'weapons of math destruction', in Cathy O'Neil's apt phrase.

The State

Capital's path to power is smoothed by the second engine of the Megamachine, the state. As a result of its capture by carefully cultivated elites, the modern state has now gone far to becoming capital's client and servant. Even its democratic institutions, although they occasionally make a bid for independence, are largely managed and manipulated by professional economic reasoners. Profitable investment is protected by a battery of legal, judicial and military apparatus. And that protection, along with the state's self-protection, is brutal when judged necessary.

By the same token, the state pushes through a bureaucratic model in all contexts, regardless of its suitability, on the assumption that 'one thing equals another'. So we have people who have only ever been managers, and know nothing about anything else, authorised (and highly paid) to tell doctors how to heal, educators how to teach, farmers how to grow food and so on. A personal calling for any of these – which one might think is a precondition for doing it well, or even at all – is now regarded as hopelessly old-fashioned, although useful as a way to keep people working despite low pay and contemptuous conditions. And as if to justify this travesty, all are forced to spend more and more time with a computer instead of their rightful primary activity (in the case of American doctors, according to a 2016 survey, now twice as long as actually seeing patients).

The disenchanting results of the modern state can be seen in the streets, bleached white and lifeless by financial acidification, of every city in the overdeveloped world. Thanks to greedy private landlords, ruthless developers, egomaniacal architects and corporations (recently joined by universities copying corporations) – all protected by pliant states – local and independent shops, traditional and useful livelihoods and affordable housing are everywhere disappearing, replaced by the anonymous banks, boring chain stores and expensively ugly houses and flats of the lords, and other servants, of capital.

The most deeply enchanting shops, for example, are the most

gone. To the best of my knowledge there are none at all left in New York or London, and very few now in Paris or Amsterdam or Florence – although maybe a few in Venice – like these, described by Bruno Schulz, which I can almost remember:

> Their dimly lit, dark, and formal interiors were redolent of the deep odor of dyes, sealing wax, incense, the aroma of distant lands and rare materials. You could find Bengal lights there, magic boxes, stamps of long-vanished countries, Chinese decals, indigo, colophony from Malabar, the eggs of exotic insects, parrots, toucans, live salamanders and basilisks, mandrake root, windup toys from Nuremberg, homunculi in flowerpots, microscopes and telescopes, and above all, rare and unusual books, old folios full of the strangest etchings and stunning stories.

Any criticism of the Megamachine is often attacked by its intellectual and cultural enforcers as conservative, nostalgic, escapist and so on. They treat 'conservative' – a desire to conserve what still works and is good – as if it meant 'reactionary'. They pretend that nostalgia can't be empowering, and they are determined that prisoners shouldn't dream of life beyond their walls, as long as those walls are sufficiently modern. As Tolkien (himself the butt of high modernist ire) writes, 'In using escape in this way the critics have chosen the wrong word, and, what is more, they are confusing, not always by sincere error, the Escape of the Prisoner with the Flight of the Deserter. Just so a Party-spokesman might have labelled departure from the misery of the Führer's or any other Reich and even criticism of it as treachery'.

10. Technoscience

Technoscience is a particular enemy of enchantment. By 'technoscience' I mean that part of modern science which is now indistinguishable from technology, and which works closely together with capital and the state. Corporations fund scientific research in return for products it can sell, and the state protects it. Except when it becomes overwhelming, public resistance to nuclear power stations, genetically modified organisms, artificial biological freakery and so on is defined as a public relations problem. The result is what Chesterton, an acute critic of modernity, calls 'progress without hope'.

I am naturally very grateful for antibiotics, anaesthetics, advanced dentistry, modern hygiene and plumbing. But are they really a complete package with nuclear energy, smart bombs, agribusiness and so on – not to mention fake news, hyper-conspiracy theories and revenge porn? Must we really accept all or nothing? And can we please stop pretending that there have been no costs or losses? For true enchantment is high on that list.

Fortunately, there are still some sciences that have not been wholly colonised by capital and can therefore provide some resistance to its rule: parts of ecology, climate science, renewable energy, complementary medicine and a few others. Most research in astronomy and much in physics also remains free of pressure to provide. These disciplines can still be inspired by wonder and defend it, even if they are institutionally averse to explicitly acknowledging its importance. They also retain the humility of science properly so-called, which admits its own limitations.

None of this applies to scientism, the ideology of technoscience. Its distinguishing mark is relentless nothing-buttery – a disenchanting one-size-fits-all metric – and its advocates claim the right to adjudicate on all matters, if not indeed to determine which questions are allowed. This is not, of course, a scientific choice. It cannot be, since the question 'Is science the best (or only) way to answer all questions?' cannot be answered scientifically without already assuming its truth and value, when that is just what is in question.

Technoscience now functions as the third integral engine of the modern Megamachine. Concerned with prediction, control and manipulation, it is conducted by teams of researchers financed by private capital, whether directly or indirectly through universities, seeking a return on its investment. This fact dictates the fields of research, the methods used and sometimes even the results, especially in developing new technologies for corporations to collect and analyse data, military applications, energy, pharmaceuticals, the 'food' industry and new ways to survey and control populations.

Founding Fathers

None of this would surprise anyone who was already aware of the formative origins of modern science. The fathers of the seventeenth-century Scientific Revolution were quite open about their hostility to enchantment and its pre-conditions in life. René Descartes declared that since 'there exists nothing in the whole of nature which cannot be explained in terms of purely corporeal causes totally devoid of mind and thought', people should learn to 'see nothing whose cause they cannot easily understand, nor anything that gives them any cause to marvel'. Or in Daniel Dennett's hokey-blokey update, 'There ain't no magic here. Just stage magic'.

Galileo Galilei, updating Plato, dismissed the entire sensual world of qualities – the living world we actually experience, in which enchantment is possible – as 'secondary', an inferior derivative of the single, uniform and universal 'primary' world, which is accessible only through experiment and mathematics.

Francis Bacon sought a single *scientia universalis* and advocated putting nature, figured as a woman, 'under constraint', to be 'vexed', 'pierced' and 'put to the question', that is, interrogated under torture. 'Conquer and subdue Nature with all her children, bind her to your service and make her your slave,' because the resulting knowledge 'itself is power'. There is no place for mere wonder in the 'human empire' that he craved.

It is very important not to accept such assertions at face value – that is, as scientific, objective or factual descriptions or (the next step) explanations of how things actually are. They are nothing of the sort, but rather metaphysical, ideological and political interventions, intended to help *create* the kind of world they say it is. As such, they evince another affinity with magic, which involves just the same sort of interventions. The connection is the exercise of will, through programme and system, to remake the world in our own image, where 'our' refers to a very small and select club in which analytically clever but socially inept men seem to figure highly.

There is a curious paradox here. Individual working scientists are usually well aware of the limits of science, including the way its undoubted successes are paid for by severely limiting the scope of its attention. Yet in the ethos of modern science as a whole, there is intense hostility to the idea of self-limiting, and translated into the point about analysis as disguised intervention, what this really means is that science ultimately recognises no limit to its right and power to completely remake the world, including ourselves.

That attitude has seeped deeply into our culture. Yet the assumption that 'If a thing can be done, it must be done' is, as Tolkien points out, 'wholly false'. Indeed, that way madness lies, as it always does in the absence of any meaningful limits. And madness, whether collective or individual, is never enchanting. On the contrary, it is deeply, terrifyingly boring.

The modes and values of the Scientific Revolution still dominate in the modern ascendency of laboratory biology. Like earlier forms of scientific naturalism, the theory of natural selection seeks to bring all aspects of life and experience under a single rule. In its most popular 'selectionist' version, it goes well beyond what Darwin suggested. Everything is supposedly subject to the iron law of survival, and the only kind of value left is 'fitness'. Such a ruthlessly disenchanting perspective leaves no room for concrete magic or irreducible intrinsic value. Once committed to the belief all things can be mastered by calculation, anything that resists is simply excluded from 'all things'.

Along with cognitive psychology and neuroscience, the theory of natural selection is now everywhere. It frames important public issues and informs mainstream politics and economics, while its speculative just-so stories are widely culturally disseminated and pass largely unchallenged. Thus Proust is patronised as a neuroscientist *avant la letter*, the medieval mystic Hildegard of Bingen is chided for confusing the effects of her migraines with the architecture of heaven (which she 'believed' existed but we 'know' doesn't), and the incomparable Paleolithic art of Lascaux is reduced to neurological epiphenomena. Such self-assurance, not to say self-importance!

A Philosophy of Death

The roots of technoscientific naturalism and scientism lie further back than the Scientific Revolution. There are principally two. The obvious one is Christian monotheism, whose commitment to a single universal truth we have already discussed. As modern science developed, a material version of truth eventually replaced God, scientific laws replaced revelation and technicians replaced theologians, but the underlying mode was left intact. So too was Christianity's antagonistic energy as a counter-religion to the human religious default (if you'll pardon the metaphor) of animism. Secular scientific naturalists have long attacked their opponents as 'superstitious' but they took the insult from Protestants attacking Catholics as pagan. It was no great stretch.

The second root is classical Greek philosophy. Plato was strongly influenced by the earlier philosopher Parmenides, who had made a radical distinction between Being – a singular, perfect, unchanging, unmoving world which is disembodied, contextless and unchanging – and the world of becoming: the sensuous, fecund and therefore female Earth and all its bodily creatures, subject to ceaseless generation, growth, decay and disappearance. He boldly identified Being with Truth, and therefore with thought: 'to be and to think are the same thing'. That leaves the world we actually know as non-Being, which therefore not only doesn't really exist but cannot even be thought.

The resulting imperative is to never stop asking, is this (whatever it may be) true or false? And the effect is to split concrete magic into these two halves. The key questions then become epistemological: how do we know what really is? And is there a sure way to distinguish between what is true, and therefore is, and what is false, and therefore is not? This was the invitation to the so-called scientific method.

The consequences for enchantment are dire. Relationality, perspective, ambiguity, liminality are condemned. So is the 'tensive truth' of metaphor, a new 'third thing' resulting from the bridge perceived/thrown between one thing and another. There isn't even a second thing! Ultimately only one thing, one world and one Truth is allowed.

Plato softened the blow slightly by allowing the world of appearances a limited and derivative reality as inferior and derivative copies of *logos*, the real world of Ideas. These copies or 'shadows' are the subject of myths which are believed only by the superstitious masses. In this way he identified *mythos*, the contrary of *logos*, with *doxa*, vulgar popular opinion. Homer was one of his principal targets.

Another was Heraclitus, who held that 'Everything flows and nothing abides; everything gives way and nothing stays fixed.' (The resonance with Daoism is striking.) The resultant uncertainty was unacceptable to Plato, not least because it brings into question any claims to final authority by a philosophical elite. *Logos* thus deftly positions the ceaseless change of Heraclitus's flux as illusory ephemera taken seriously only by the ignorant masses.

As we have already observed, Plato's philosophy also left

Aphrodite's love, which we identified as an exemplar of enchantment, as inferior, gross and fallible. Unlike the love between a man and a woman, or between two women, the love of a man for a beautiful boy leads his soul onwards and upwards to beauty, we are to suppose, as such and in itself. But Plato's idea of beauty has eliminated all concrete magic; it is unadulterated, as Wittgenstein pointedly remarks, by anything beautiful. Love therefore becomes instrumental, a mere ladder leading up to an Idea. As usual, Nietzsche saw the point clearly: 'the worst, most durable, and most dangerous of all errors so far was a dogmatist's error – namely, Plato's invention of the pure spirit and the good as such'.

Plato's student Aristotle, despite some interesting differences, continued and further developed the essentials of his master's teachings. Of particular relevance, he formalised the idea of Being as logical truths. These eventually became 'principles of reason', supposedly universally true, three in particular:

1. The principle of identity: something is entirely and only itself.
2. The principle of non-contradiction: nothing is, or can be, both itself and not itself (at the same time and in the same respects).
3. The principle of the excluded middle: everything is exhaustively either itself or not at all. (This is also known as *tertium non datur*: literally, 'a third (alternative) is not given'.)

These 'truths' function as laws, accompanied by penalties for non-observance, and as metaphysical assertions about the nature of reality. They express Parmenides' attempt to annihilate life in favour of Being, and along with life everything that makes enchantment possible. They are also extraordinarily implausible. There are different things in the world, and without differences it would be impossible for each kind and each individual to be itself; so life is multiple. Things also change continuously, since in time everything, in some respect and to some degree or another, is no longer, or is not yet; so life continually alters. Finally, all beings, being interdependent, both are and are not entirely themselves; so life is metaphoric.

Ironically, it isn't their rational or empirical plausibility whence Aristotle's laws draw their power. Rather they tap into the cold rage of the male wound which we discussed earlier. Auden puts his finger on it, as usual: 'There is in all males, I believe, a strong Manichean streak, an unacknowledged secret contempt for matter, both animate and inanimate'.

If that is your starting point, then, and it's power you want, Aristotle's injunctions are extremely useful. For scientific modernists, they offer the metaphysical basis of a method for ruling that defines everything as self-identical objects, which are therefore suitable to be mastered – not troublesome, independently minded subjects with their own agenda, demanding relationships. In their world (which they are busy making our world), every apparent subject is really a lifeless object which you haven't sufficiently analysed yet to realise that. Thus subjectivity and consciousness are placemarkers waiting to be reduced to 'purely physical' phenomena. Indeed, life itself is merely incompletely realised death.

In an enchanted world and condition, on the contrary, any object – even things that are technically inanimate – can turn out to be a subject. This is the great insight of animism. In practice, a stone, or star, or storm can have a personality. As much as any other kind of person, it can speak, and act, and sometimes enchant.

Plato's philosophy of death not only sought to sever reality from appearances but also from embodied life. Death is redefined as true life, because spirit is supposedly eternal. This perverse reversal entered directly into Christianity and Islam. ('To be carnally minded is death; but to be spiritually minded is life and peace'.) The goal of philosophy then becomes, in Plato's words, 'to untie the soul from the body,' leaving only 'the divine and not appearance… free of any human evil'. Notice how this conflates 'human' and 'evil'. Death is therefore to be welcomed, because then the soul will be free of the 'prison' or 'tomb' of the body and the 'cave' of the Earth. ('Praise God the open door, I ain't got no home in this world anymore'.)

I believe this philosophy is present in the worship of cyberspace as, in effect, Plato's heaven of perfect Ideas. It is not only present but in charge in the madness of the transhumanists – largely funded by Silicon Valley billionaires – who want us to join them in abandoning their bodies and the Earth and uploading their sorry souls into cyberspace, or in denying death through endless serial living, in a grotesque parody of immortality, as cyborg wraiths. What more striking confirmation could there be of another of Auden's percipient observations, that 'where, in fact or in fantasy, power is unlimited, relations with other persons and with nature vanish and the victim is condemned to an unending dialogue with himself on the subject of death, unreal, theatrical, mad'?

But these men too are utterly dependent on their aliveness, their bodies and the Earth in which, and thanks to which, they live – not to mention the women who gave birth to them. The very project to 'transcend' these things depends on them. Even to choose death, you must already be alive!

The false promise of death-as-life still circulates in the Western metaphysical imagination, not least in the scientific fantasy of mastery. Some of our leading philosophies remain ones of death, either the religious supernaturalism of extreme spiritual idealists or the scientistic nihilism of extreme materialists. Despising the Earthly life on which they depend, their followers either worship death as spiritual fulfilment or, fearing it as the absolute end, crave scientific immortality. What Tolkien says is all that is on offer, this side of the grave – 'hope without guarantees' – isn't good enough for them, and they are quite prepared to destroy what we have in the search for security.

There is one more twist to this spiral of terminal disenchantment, namely its radical misogyny. Plato's contempt for women is no secret, and all the splitting we have identified was gendered to its roots: not only between men and women, but within each person between a female Earthly body and a male spiritual soul. Aristotle continued this doctrine, allotting to men alone the power to generate souls; the woman is not the origin of life but merely a passive receptacle and temporary container. He also defined 'Man' – that is, all of humanity – as 'a rational animal'; but since reason is supposedly male, women are at best honorary humans. This is how masculinity can pose as universal and neutral.

Such misogyny is inherent in the philosophical celebration of death and denial of life, including birth, and with it, the mother. Earlier we discussed the figure of the 'dark female', birthing both life and death, at the heart of enchantment. Every human being, whether male or female, was born of woman, who was in turn born of woman, and so on back into our endless origin in the living matrix, still going on, of life on Earth. So in attempting to erase birth, the Platonic tradition effects, even requires, a symbolic matricide. And since the ultimate source of life is the Earth itself, that matricide is also ecocidal.

Bizarrely, these ancient male philosophers evince a raw envy of the female power to give birth to life, and a desire to appropriate it. What they wanted was to give birth, through philosophical reflection, to pure spiritual souls who will ascend to heaven: their *own* souls, self-created, absolutely independent and 'free'. Surely this is the ultimate destructive fantasy, and it continues in the name of biotechnology, artificial intelligence and neurophysiology. In the words of one of its bright young cheerleaders, Yuval Noah Harari:

> What we're talking about now is like a second Industrial Revolution, but the product this time will not be textiles or machines or vehicles, or even weapons. The product this time will be humans themselves. We're basically learning to produce bodies and minds. Bodies and minds are going to be the two main products of the next wave of all these changes. And if there is a gap between those that know how to produce bodies and minds and those that do not, then this is far greater than anything we saw before in history.

This sort of pronouncement is presented as cutting-edge stuff, but it's really the same old dream-cum-nightmare: a programme for male human supremacy. Harari adds menacingly that 'this time, if you're not fast enough to become part of the revolution, then you'll probably become extinct'. You've been warned.

11. Enchantment as a Way of Life

Let's see where we've been. True enchantment is sheer existential wonder at, and selfless love for, an other. Because this is not a thing but a relationship – a meeting, an encounter across a gap – neither controlling power-over nor orgasmic union-with can encompass it. It is unbiddable by our will, and it does not survive the destruction of the differences which it needs in order to transcend them. Nor does transcendence destroy boundaries, or need to.

That kind of meeting is metaphor, and metaphor is meeting. Metaphor consists, if you remember, of 'This' (whatever it might be) 'is that!' (whatever it might be), but without either this or that ceasing to be what they are. To return to an example from an earlier chapter, 'This elderly Austrian woman is a dragon!' But at the same time, she is just the former, and a dragon too is what it remains.

When this is personally realised, you too are still you, but at the same time you are also in relationship with the resulting new being and its enchantment, because the part of you that has realised its metaphoric truth is conjoined with it. Otherwise you couldn't have realised it, only perhaps imagined it. But enchantment, says one of Tolkien's definitions, is 'the realisation... of imagined wonder'. Which takes place, he adds, 'independent of the conceiving mind'. In other words, it's not merely a cognitive or (in the usual sense of the word) psychological event.

This is the dynamic of the meaning of the word 'enchantment': to find yourself inside a song, story or any narrative, even as you hear or read or hear it from the outside. The result can transform the person involved, who experiences radical enchantment as joy, potentially reordering and reorienting their life.

The other party can be anyone or anything – another human

or other animal, plant, place, artefact, story, song, idea, value –
which has a personality, so is *this* and not *that*. Or perhaps he/she/
it becomes a definite personality in the moment of meeting. In any
case, since we humans are also a particular kind of being, we have
a lot in common, so we also tend to find enchantment in certain
ways and contexts. Hence we considered enchantment in, and as,
love, art, religion, food, learning and nature. (This is not to say I
haven't missed any. Two obvious omissions are sports and humour.)

The more-than-human natural world is the ultimate source of
enchantment. More specifically, the primary sites of enchantment
are the bodymind, the female, and the Earth. But these are not to
be understood as modernity has defined them for its own purposes.
The bodymind is not a machine but a subject as much as it is an
object. The female is not an essence but an irreducible inflection of
being human, defining and defined by its male counterpole. And
nature is not an aggregate of inert natural resources for humans
but the living more-than-human world.

In all three interlinked domains, enchantment returns us to a
state of mind, and condition of the world, as undivided concrete
magic: equally natural and cultural, material and spiritual,
physical and mental, inner and outer. Thus it ignores the pieties
of disenchanted modernism, no matter how ingrained, and they
have no purchase while it lasts.

It follows that you cannot understand wonder if your starting-
point is that ultra-modernist piety, a radical split between mind
and matter. It cannot survive being reduced to something that
is 'physical' – neurophysiology, mostly – nor something that is
'mental', that is, a cognitive state of mind, belief, representation
and so on. As Wittgenstein says, 'Physiological life is of course
not "Life." And neither is psychological life. Life is the world'.
Enchantment is a matter of life and the world, including (but far
from only) us. And since the world is precisely 'your countless soul',
it is equally inner and outer.

Then one finds oneself in *Faërie*. But because of its concrete
dimension, enchantment, like love, lasts forever only while it's
happening, which is never permanently or completely; humans

cannot live long in *Faërie*. In that sense, leave-taking is present from the start, so there is often a melancholy undertow in enchantment, a pre-emptive nostalgia. But given its inseparability from the wonder of enchantment, it can be experienced as 'a delicious melancholy' – what Julian Green found in his beloved Paris – or 'sweet melancholy': Jan Morris describing Trieste. With luck, the joy of radical enchantment is even seasoned with a sadness that is, as Tolkien puts it, 'blessed and without bitterness'. (There is a pure musical expression of this quality, by the way: the third movement of Beethoven's string quartet Opus 132.)

Not surprisingly, the primary sites of enchantment are also primary targets for the Megamachine, whose assignment is to realise the rational mastery of nature. So it tries to disenchant them by invading, colonising and controlling them. In the course of that attempt, it replaces wonder with glamour, which can be controlled and encourages false enchantment, the desire to possess or be possessed, which the Megamachine then offers to satisfy.

Now the systematic disenchantment of the world which I have described really is pretty bad. The net is spreading, the meshes are thickening and the gaps are shrinking. I guess you can still live off-grid, but it's a lot harder than it used to be. No wonder Weber called modernity an 'iron cage'. But if we look around, it's undeniable that we also see people falling in love, fighting for other animals and natural places, being carried away by beautiful music and so on. Evidently enchantment is still happening. Chesterton is right: 'The world will never starve for want of wonders, but only for want of wonder'.

Indeed, I believe that as the kind of being we are – ensouled and embodied, emplaced and ecological – enchantment is our birthright, and will continue to be for as long as we exist. In this sense, it sets a limit to the modern drive for mastery, including self-mastery, which is why true believers in modernism despise and mock it. (The giveaway is often when humour is used aggressively. Personally, I like my humour funny, not weaponised.) That limit cannot be overcome without our own destruction. 'The disenchantment of the world' is therefore an important half-truth. In the words of the artist Etel Adnan, enchantment is both 'vulnerable and indestructible'.

On the night of 19 May 1942, a BBC sound engineer was recording a nightingale singing in a Surrey garden when, increasing to a roar before slowly dying away, there came the sound of waves of bombers flying overhead, on their way to Germany. The nightingale sang gorgeously on regardless. The song didn't stop the war, and the war didn't stop the song. But there is no room for complacency; since 1997, thanks to 'development', the number of nightingales in the British Isles has declined by 60%.

I'm also reminded of Peter Cook's sardonic praise, when opening a comedy club in Soho, London in 1961, of 'those wonderful Berlin cabarets which did so much to stop the rise of Hitler and prevent the outbreak of the Second World War'. Indeed! But this is not an argument against opening comedy clubs. God knows, we need a few laughs.

Another way to understand the paradox of vulnerable-and-indestructible is to recall the inherent passingness of enchantment. Thus childhood is continually becoming adult (or worse, Adult); the wild countryside is constantly falling to ugly urban sprawl; the Elves are always passing over the Sea, leaving us standing in the dark on the shore of Middle-earth in the Age of Men. (There are many accounts, in addition to Tolkien's, which blend just these themes and convey the same bittersweet delight. Karen Blixen's *Out of Africa* is one, Gerald Durrell's *My Family and Other Animals* another.)

So maybe its precarious, fugitive condition in the modern world reflects a more existential truth: although enchantment is endless, it is also true that there is less of it all the time. Or, to be slightly more precise, there are steadily more times when and places where it isn't happening, while simultaneously, in *Faërie* – wherever and whenever that happens to be – there is as much as ever.

There have been times when enchantment was in the cultural ascendency, although never unmixed or for very long: the Italian Renaissance; the Belle Époque, straddling either side of the start of the twentieth century; and the late 1960s and very early 70s, for choice. Glittering baubles all, to be sure, but how we remember them! Indeed, how they have stayed with us, their apparent evanescence notwithstanding. Millions are still entranced by Leonardo, Michelangelo, Raphael and the phalanx of other Italian masters of the late fifteenth and early sixteenth centuries. The same is true of Impressionism, the Arts and Crafts Movement, and Art Nouveau, while the music of the 60s, in all it delicate or anarchic glory, will be resonate as long as people are still listening.

There are also some cultures where enchantment has an honoured place, although never unchallenged. I am thinking of France, Italy and Japan, for example. The context is usually longstanding traditions of art which are taken seriously; but often also, significantly, of food. In the background is a relationship to the natural world, neither as threatening non-human wilderness nor as human-ruled and compliant, but as powerful maternal matrix, both practical and spiritual, which is to be treated respectfully. In the various convivial relationships defined by these spheres, there is scope for enchantment to flourish. Conversely, of course, there are many cultures where the contrary is true, relatively speaking, so enchantment leads a furtive, impoverished life.

A Way of Life?

We know that permanent and complete enchantment is not an option. Nor can it be accomplished by an act of will, no matter how well-intentioned. ('I will now re-enchant the world'. Really?) Some people think it can be used for progressive purposes, but enchantment cannot be used at all; it really is unbiddable. So the most and best one can do is to create, whether individually or collectively, inviting conditions for enchantment in whatever field and walk of life, and then let *it* do its thing, perform its wonders if and as it will. You cannot legislate for the effects.

Assuming one values enchantment, the question then becomes, what kind of relationship with it may we best have? Take, for example, the famous episode in Proust's great work in which the narrator, upon tasting a madeleine biscuit dipped in tea, finds himself both an adult in his Paris apartment and simultaneously a child in his aunt's house in Combray. This is a classic experience of enchantment and it is indeed one of the centerpieces of his lifework, but it is not its principal subject. That is rather the struggle to make and support a way of life in which such experiences may fully flower and impart their deepest meanings.

How then may enchantment come to have an honoured place in one's life, as a valued part of it? The minimum requirement is surely a non-possessive love of the other for its intrinsic value, for its own sake, which is willing to just let it be. That includes resisting the impulse to meddle, interfere and control. Equally, one must be able to do without enchantment in its absence. To tolerate being back in the dry and leafless world is true maturity and a *sine qua non* for a healthy relationship with enchantment if and when it does happen.

Meanwhile, one can leave the door to enchantment open, wherever and whenever it offers itself, and practise doing so. This habit overlaps with animism, which counsels one to remain open to agency and subjectivity, regardless of whose. It also resonates with what Zwicky calls 'the domestic'. Situated between pure lyric enchantment, on the one hand, and technological manipulation on the other, the domestic in this sense is where we actually live.

Beyond that, another possibility suggests itself: one could try to work with enchantment, to encourage it, and to learn from whatever it has to show us. I have already suggested that it partly reveals and partly creates deep truths about ourselves and the world. (These should not be confused with eternal universal axioms that supposedly require no participation to be true.)

Here, at last, the will can be fully involved without driving enchantment away. Indeed, it may actually be needed. Isn't it a vital part of what every true artist does? But what we're talking about isn't limited to those who work with paint or notes or words. It includes anyone who wants to work with their own life and world, as enchantment reveals/creates it.

Can this work be further specified? Perhaps. The process of

enchantment, it seems to me, is two-fold. One, the senses are fully engaged with the concrete and therefore sensuous dimension of one's precise circumstances. Two, the imagination is fully engaged with the inner lining and depth of the concrete, not as its opposite but as its mysterious meaning which would otherwise not exist. Imagination in this sense means the opposite of what is usually meant by 'fantasy'. It is rather an organ of perception. As Mark Twain says, 'you can't depend on your eyes when your imagination is out of focus'.

What then is the imagination apprehending? It must be something that is not given directly to the other senses, yet is in what they perceive. That could be a past that is apparently no longer happening but has brought about this moment, or a future that hasn't happened yet but is implicit in it, or another place, not concretely present but with which this place is reciprocally implicated, as the city is with the wilderness or the mountains with the plain. When the imagination works together with sensuous perception in this way – stereoscopically, as it were – what results is a depth that can come about in no other way.

This shows the futility, not to mention banality, of the injunction to 'Be here now', when it is understood to mean sticking to one's exact circumstances with an absolute minimum of imagination. One cannot be *in* a moment, or a place, if it's flat. And if the creative imagination is suppressed rather than engaged, that will be the effect. (As Bateson once remarked of the Rorschach ink blot diagnostic test, if you see *only* a blot of ink then you really are sick.)

It may also be that the imagination can simply find no way in: when a situation is, as Kravis says, 'so ordinary it's unreachable'. This is what happens to me in the Canadian prairies, where I was born. For whatever reasons, its immensity has remained stubbornly two-dimensional, opaque and impenetrable, the senses revealing only a flimsy veil over an existential void. It's not surprising that I found my way to Europe. Perhaps if I had had access to local Cree and Ojibwe stories they might have helped me get into the land; but for someone like me then, that wasn't really an option.

The same phenomenon of the senses including imagination

should help put paid to another misguided notion, namely that you can divide experience into what is real, meaning material, and what is 'only' a metaphor. Life is material ('concrete') all the way 'up' and metaphoric ('magic') all the way 'down'. Literal truth – 'The stone is hard', say – is a foundational metaphor, connecting, out of many other possibilities, 'stone' with 'hardness'. The double action of enchantment, sensuous and imaginative, is a particularly intense realisation of a more general truth: that in the words of a poem by Wallace Stevens, 'reality is an activity of the most august imagination'.

What might be the ultimate enchantment? Not final, complete or eternal, of course, but the deepest and most wondrous? I suggest it is what Shunryu Suzuki, in a felicitous phrase, calls 'things-as-it-is': the exact concrete circumstances, including their incarnate meaning, of actually being alive here and now, without any wilfulness, method or programme. Things-as-it-is are, and is, a gift. Or grace, if you prefer.

But this gift goes beyond simple acceptance. We are thinking, feeling and willing beings. What can we do beyond making enchantment welcome? We can attend to it, allow it to happen, and help the wonder of the world to become real. Then we become real in turn.

Endnotes

Opening epigraph

Shunryu Suzuki: *Zen Mind, Beginner's Mind* (New York: Weatherhill, 1970): 61.

1. Introduction

p. 7

Definition: I have borrowed this point from Paul Valéry ('Indefinable is essential to the definition'), quoted by W.H. Auden: *The Complete Works of W.H. Auden, Prose*, Vol. 4, ed. Edward Mendelson (Princeton: Princeton University Press, 2015): 479.

p. 8

Textiles: Gensho Sasakura, *Tsutsugaki Textiles of Japan* (Kyoto: Shikosha, 1987).

Perfumes: Luca Turin and Tania Sanchez, *Perfumes: The Guide* (London: Profile, 2009): 404.

Motorcycles: Melissa Holbrook Pierson, *The Perfect Vehicle* (London: Granta, 1997): 236. (With thanks to Bernard Eccles.)

Undeserved suffering: Max Weber, H.H. Gerth and C. Wright Mills (eds), *From Max Weber: Essays in Sociology* (London: Routledge, 1991): 122.

Disenchantment of the world: Weber: 155.

p. 9

The farther in you go: John Crowley, *Little, Big* (London: Victor Gollancz, 1982): 43.

Dionysian/Apollonian: I have borrowed this polarity from Nietzsche's *The Birth of Tragedy* but used it for my own purposes, just as he did. I don't pretend to have represented these gods adequately thereby.

p. 10

Paradoxically the self: Ethel Spector Person, *Dreams of Love and Fateful Encounters. The Power of Romantic Passion* (Washington D.C.: American Psychiatric Publishing Inc., 2007): 39.

Auden: *Prose*, Vol. 6: 343. Compare George MacDonald, whom Auden also quotes on the same page: 'there can be no oneness where there is only one.'

p. 11

'Theôria': see Andrea Wilson Nightingale, *Spectacles of Truth in Classical Greek Philosophy. Theoria in its Cultural Context* (Cambridge University Press, 2004).

Description alone: Ludwig Wittgenstein, *Philosophical Investigations*, transl. G.E.M. Anscombe (Oxford: Blackwell, 2001): 40e (proposition 109).

2. The Dynamics of Enchantment

p.13

True vs false enchantment: W.H. Auden, *A Certain World: A Commonplace Book* (New York: The Viking Press, 1970): 149.

Love and respect: J.R.R. Tolkien, *Smith of Wootton Major*, extended edition, ed. Verlyn Flieger (London: HarperCollins, 2005): 101.

p.14

The country leaving: Karen Blixen, *Out of Africa* (New York: Random House, 1970 [1937]): 381.

Wittgenstein: quoted (from the *Tractatus Logico-Philosophicus*) in Jan Zwicky, *Wittgenstein Elegies* (Toronto: Brick Books, 2015): 54.

Faërie: J.R.R. Tolkien, 'On Fairy-Stories' (henceforth 'OFS'), pp. 9–73 in *Tree and Leaf* (London: Unwin Hyman, 1988 [1964]): 14. For a recent edition, see Verlyn Flieger and Douglas A. Anderson (eds), *Tolkien on Fairy-stories*, expanded edition, with commentary and notes (London: HarperCollins, 2008).

p.15

Only from the train: Elizabeth Bowen, *A Time in Rome* (London: Vintage Books, 2010 [1959]): 242.

In the manner of a gift: William James, 'The Dilemma of Determinism', in *The Will to Believe and Other Essays in Popular Philosophy* (London: Longman, 1897): 154.

p.16

Eugen Rosenstock-Huessy: quoted in Auden, *Prose*, Vol. 6: 643.

Ten Steps: But I know of two popular books on enchantment with self-help implications, both good: Thomas Moore, *The Re-Enchantment of Everyday Life* (New York: HarperPerennial, 1997) and Sharon Blackie, *The Enchanted Life* (Tewksbury: September Publishing, 2018).

Fearless receptivity: Freya Stark, *Perseus in the Wind* (London: I.B. Tauris, 2013 [1948]): 107.

Negative capability: John Keats, letter to George and Thomas Keats (December 1817).

p.17

More-than-human: David Abram, *The Spell of the Sensuous* (New York: Vintage Books, 1997).

Concrete magic: Max Weber: 282. See Gregory Bateson's closely parallel discussion in chapter 5, 'Neither Supernatural nor Mechanical', in Gregory Bateson and Mary Catherine Bateson, *Angels Fear. An Investigation into the Nature and Meaning of the Sacred* (London: Rider, 1987).

Capture something: Michael Longley, in *The Irish Times* (11.1.92).

p.18

The idea God had: Blixen, *Out of Africa*: 261.

An idea that is not: Maurice Merleau-Ponty, *The Visible and the Invisible*, ed. Claude Lefort and transl. Alphonso Lingis (Evanston: Northwestern University Press, 1968): 149.

Radiant specificity: Jan Zwicky, *Lyric Philosophy* (Toronto: University of Toronto Press, 1992): 536.

Plato seems to have made: Aldous Huxley, *The Doors of Perception and Heaven and Hell* (Harmondsworth: Penguin, 1959): 17.

p.19

Luminous moment and I found it impossible: Patrick Leigh Fermor, *A Time of Gifts* (London: John Murray, 2004 [1977]): 355, 358.

p.20

It seemed to him: J.R.R. Tolkien, *The Lord of the Rings*, Vol. 1: *The Fellowship of the Ring*

(London: George Allen & Unwin, 1954): Bk 2, ch. 6.

Dreaming: see e.g. Deborah Bird Rose, *Reports from a Wild Country: Ethics for Decolonisation* (Sydney: University of New South Wales Press, 2004): 54–57 and *passim*.

The moment of your greatest joy: cf.Joanna Newsom, 'Time, as a Symptom', from the album *Divers* (2015).

p.21

Rational pursuit: phrase taken from Val Plumwood, *Feminism and the Mastery of Nature* (London: Routledge: 1993).

Modernity: see my 'Enchantment and Modernity', *PAN: Philosophy, Activism, Nature* 12 (2012) 76–89, accessible at http://www.patrickcurry.co.uk/papers/Enchantment%20and%20Modernity%20for%20PAN.pdf

'Your countless soul': Judy Kravis, *these women* (Garravagh: A Boreen Book, 2018): 'sea spinach' [n.p.].

p.22

Realisation of imagined: J.R.R. Tolkien, OFS: 37.

In the presence: Wallace Stevens, *Collected Poetry and Prose*, ed. Frank Kermode and Joan Richardson (New York: Library of America, 1997): 905.

p.23

Nothing further to seek: Lucien Lévy-Bruhl, *The Notebooks on Primitive Mentality*, transl. Lilian A. Clare (Harper & Row, 1975): 109.

Ideas and emotions: Sean Kane, *Wisdom of the Mythtellers*, 2nd ed. (Peterborough: Broadview Press, 1998): 50.

p.24

On Hermes: I have benefitted from, among other sources, the speculations of Russell Hoban in *The Moment Under the Moment. Stories, a Libretto, Essays and Sketches* (London: Jonathan Cape, 1992):

p.25

On metaphor: see Paul Ricoeur, *The Rule of Metaphor: The Creation of Meaning in Language*, transl. Robert Czerny (London: Routledge, 2003).

p.26

Syllogism in grass: Bateson and Bateson, *Angels Fear*: 26–27.

Dark female, *Daodejing: "Making This Life Significant": A Philosophical Translation*, transl. and ed. Roger T. Ames and David L. Hall (New York: Ballantine Books, 2003): 85.

3. Love

p.27

All of a sudden: Alain-Fournier, *Towards the Lost Domain: Letters from London 1905*, transl. W.J. Strachan (Manchester: Carcanet, 1986): 208, 210–12.

Annabelle paused: Margery Allingham, *Hide My Eyes* (London: Penguin, 1960): 37–38.

p.28

Ono no Komachi: *The Ink Dark Moon: Love Poems by Ono no Komachi and Izumi Shikibu*, transl. Jane Hirshfield with Mariko Aratani (New York: Vintage Books, 1990): 55.

p.29

O toi: taken from Cyril Connolly, *The Unquiet Grave: A Word Cycle by Palinurus* (New York: Persea Books, 1981 [1951]): 79–80.

Weber: *From Max Weber*: 348.

Proust: *Swann in Love*, transl. Brian Nelson (Oxford: Oxford University Press, 2017): 148, 178.

Boorishness: *Swann*: 181.

p.30

Thomas Mann: *Death in Venice and Other Stories*, ed. David Luke (London: Vintage, 1988): 223. The influence of the Goethe incident is asserted by Auden, *Prose*, Vol. 6: 457.

Goethe's infatuation: one is also forcibly reminded of William Hazlitt and Sarah Walker; see Jon Cook, *Hazlitt in Love: A Fatal Attachment* (London: Short Books, 2007).

Roberto Calasso: *The Marriage of Cadmus and Harmony*, transl. Tim Parks (London: Jonathan Cape, 1988): 19.

On Aphrodite: see Paul Friedrich, *The Meaning of Aphrodite* (Chicago: University of Chicago Press, 1978) and Geoffrey Grigson, *The Goddess of Love: The Birth, Triumph, Death and Return of Aphrodite* (London: Constable, 1976). Both are excellent.

p.31

Montaigne: Michel de Montaigne, *The Complete Essays*, transl. M.A. Screech (London: Penguin, 1993): 1269.

p.32

Love gives itself: Ginette Paris, *Pagan Meditations. Aphrodite, Hestia, Artemis* (Dallas: Spring Publications, 1986): 65.

Smile: William Blake, *Complete Writings*: 423.

Robert Louis Stevenson, *An Apology for Idlers* (London: Penguin Books, 2009): 36.

p.35

Comprehensive force: Clive James, *Cultural Amnesia. Notes in the Margin of my Time* (London: Picador, 2007): 19.

p.37

Need for knowledge: Friedrich Nietzsche, *The Gay Science*, section 355.

p.38

State of grace: Gabriel García Márquez, *Love in the Time of Cholera*, transl. Edith Grossman (New York: Alfred A. Knopf, 1988): 293.

4. Art

p.44

'Rationalisation': Weber: 155.

By flight: D.W. Winnicott, *Playing and Reality* (London: Routledge, 2005): 7.

p.45

What the real garden: C.S. Lewis, from *Surprised by Joy* (With thanks to Alf Seegert.)

p.46

'Rotten with perfection': Kenneth Burke, quoted in Herbert W. Simons and Trevor Melia (eds), *The Legacy of Kenneth Burke* (Madison: University of Wisconsin Press, 1989): 263.

p.47

Pullman: see my essay 'The Third Road: Faërie in Hypermodernity', in Graham Harvey (ed.), *The Handbook of Animism* (Durham: Acumen, 2013) pp. 468–478; accessible at http://www.patrickcurry.co.uk/papers/The%20Third%20Road%20Harvard.pdf

p.48

Art of storytelling: Walter Benjamin, 'The Storyteller', pp. 83–109 in *Illuminations*, ed. Hannah Arendt (New York: Schocken Books, 1969): 87, 101, 102.

Lifelong admirer: for Auden on Tolkien's work, see the former's *Prose*, 3: 489–99 and 491–94; 4: 3–6 and 369–73; 5: 331–35 and 369–73.

Mythopoeic imagination: W.H. Auden, *The Complete Works of W.H. Auden*, Vol. 3: *Prose*, ed. Edward Mendelson (London: Faber and Faber, 2008): 322.

p.49

Second naïveté: Paul Ricoeur, *The Symbolism of Evil*, transl. Emerson Buchanen (Boston: Beacon Press, 1967): 351.

Scholar of the heart: Richard Wilbur, 'Poetry and Happiness', pp. 469–89 in Donald Hall (ed.), *Claims for Poetry* (Ann Arbor: The University of Michigan Press, 1982): 479–80.

Once almost identical: see J.S. Morrison, 'The Classical World', pp. 87–114 in Michael Loewe and Carmen Blacker (eds), *Oracles and Divination* (Boulder: Shambhala, 1981): 95.

Essential quality of poetry: D.H. Lawrence, 'Chaos in Poetry', in *Exchanges*, December 1929; republished as an introduction to Harry Crosby, *Chariot of the Sun* (Paris: Black Sun Press, 1931): 234. (Thanks to Victor Postnikov.)

p.51

All art aspires: Walter Pater, in the 3rd edition (1888) of his *Studies in the History of the Renaissance*.

p.52

'Who look at the stage as if…': Bertold Brecht, quoted in Rita Felski, *Uses of Literature* (Oxford: Blackwell, 2008): 56.

'Why is art beautiful?': Fernando Pessoa, *The Book of Disquiet*, transl. Richard Zenith (London: Penguin, 2002): 278.

'A reason for everything': Wallace Stevens, *The Necessary Angel: Essays on Reality and the Imagination* (London: Faber and Faber, 1960): 167.

'You can't vandalize something': Dinos Chapman, quoted in Ben Lerner, 'Damage Control: The modern art world's tyranny of price', *Harper's Magazine* (Dec. 2013) pp. 43–49: 48.

p.54

Fetishizing difficulty for its own sake, etc.: the essays of Susan Sontag are as good an example as any of this.

'His majestic baubles': Peter Schjeldahl, 'Spot On', *The New Yorker* (23.1.12) 84–85.

p.55

'Decades later': Pierre Schaeffer, in David Rothenberg and Marta Ulvaeus (eds), *The Book of Music and Nature: An Anthology of Sounds, Words, Thoughts* (Middletown: Wesleyan University Press, 2001), pp. 34–43: 42.

'A gift': Susan Tomes, *Out of Silence. A Pianist's Yearbook* (Woodbridge: The Boydell Press, 2010): 276.

5. Religion

p.59

Wittgenstein: *Culture and Value*, rev. 2nd ed. (Oxford: Blackwell, 1998): 10e.

In the gutter: one of Oscar Wilde's *aperçus*.

p.62

Monotheism: see Jan Assmann, *The Price of Monotheism*, transl. Robert Savage (Stanford: Stanford University Press, 2010). Of historical treatments, see, e.g., Jonathan Kirsch, *God Against the Gods: The History of the War between Monotheism and Polytheism* (New York: Penguin, 2004); Rodney Stark, *One True God. Historical Consequences of Monotheism* (Princeton: Princeton University Press, 2001); and Regina M. Schwartz, *The Curse of Cain: The Violent Legacy of Monotheism* (Chicago: University of Chicago Press, 1997).

Barbara Herrnstein Smith: *Contingencies of Value. Alternative Perspectives for Critical Theory* (Cambridge MA: Harvard University Press, 1988): 179.

p.64

Knowledge or belief: Weber: 139.

6. Food and Drink

p.69

We ate: M.F.K. Fisher, from *Gastronomy Recalled...* (1968), quoted in *The New Yorker* (21/28.2.2000).

p.70

The peel: Elizabeth Bowen, *A Time in Rome*: 43–44.

The taste: Stephen L. Kaplan, from Lennox Morrison, 'Omnivore', *Metropolitan* (n.d.) pp. 35–38.

p.71

When you condemn: Michel Serres, *The Five Senses: A Philosophy of Mingled Bodies*, transl. Margaret Sankey and Peter Cowley (London: Continuum, 2008): 326.

Foodlike: from Michael Pollan, *In Defense of Food* (New York: Penguin, 2009).

p.72

Simply by sipping: Patrick Leigh Fermor, *Gifts*: 65.

Finnish language: J.R.R. Tolkien, *The Letters of J.R.R. Tolkien*, ed. Humphrey Carpenter and Christopher Tolkien (London: HarperCollins, 2006): 214 (Letter 163).

7. Learning

p.73

Coming of evening: Niccolò Machiavelli, *The Prince, selections from The Discourse and other writings*, ed. John Plamenatz (London: Fontana/Collins, 1972): 360. (Translations vary slightly.)

Aristocracy: John Ruskin, from *Marcel Proust and John Ruskin, On Reading*, ed. and transl. Damion Searls (London: Hesperus Press, 2011): 58.

Seriousness: Friedrich Nietzsche, *Beyond Good and Evil* (Harmondsworth: Penguin Books, 1973): 94.

p.74

Personally affected: see Geoffrey Cornelius, "Verity and the Question of Primary and Secondary Scholarship in Astrology", pp. 103-113 in Nicholas Campion, Patrick Curry and Michael York (eds), *Astrology and the Academy* (Bristol: Cinnabar Books, 2004).

Auden: *Prose*, Vol. 5: 416.

p.75

Some can: Wittgenstein, *Investigations*: 193 e.

It never seems: Ruskin, 58.

Zweig: *Montaigne*, transl. Will Stone (London: Pushkin Press, 2015): 52.

p.76

Connolly: *Unquiet Grave*: 58. Cf. Freya Stark, *The Zodiac Arch* (London: I.B. Tauris & Co, 2014), p. 205, on 'the feeling of well-being and intimacy' she found in *Unquiet Grave*.

The real university: J.M. Coetzee, *Diary of a Bad Year* (London: Vintage, 2008): 36.

p.77

Wisdom of uncertainty: Milan Kundera, *The Art of the Novel* (London: Faber and Faber, 1990).

Do I contradict: Walt Whitman, from 'Song of Myself'.

The opposite: Niels Bohr, quoted by Hans Bohr in Stefan Rozental (ed.), *Niels Bohr: His Life and Work* (New York: Wiley, 1967): 328. See also Philip Wheelwright, *Metaphor and Reality* (Bloomington: Indian University Press, 1962).

Methodolatry: borrowed from Mary Midgley.

8. Nature

p.79

On enchantment is/as nature, see Haydn Washington, *A Sense of Wonder Towards Nature* (Abingdon: Routledge, 2019).

Wood: (My adapted translation) Hans Børli, from *Med øks og lyre: Blar av en tømmerhuggers dagbok* (Oslo: Aschenhoug, 1988), quoted in Lars Mytting, *Norwegian Wood*, transl. Robert Ferguson (London: Maclehose Press, 2015), n.p. (With thanks to Suzanna Saumarez.)

Farmer: *Essays of E.B. White* (New York: Harper & Row, 1977): 274.

p.80

George Orwell: *Collected Essays, Journalism and Letters*, Vol. 4, ed. Sonia Orwell and Ian Angus (Harmondsworth: Penguin, 1970): 'Some Thoughts on the Common Toad' (171–175): 175.

The story about Aron and Weil is told by Adam Zagajewski in *Slight Exaggeration*, transl. Clare Cavanagh (New York: Farrar, Straus and Giroux, 2011): 134. I would add that I find Weil's religious asceticism repugnant. It violently disrespects the gift of embodied and potentially enchanted life for reasons which Montaigne, in his final essays, discusses and rejects.

p.81

Humanus: see Sean Kane, 'Humanus', *Green Letters: Studies in Ecocriticism* 13 (Winter 2010) 22–34.

Style of being: Maurice Merleau-Ponty, *Visible*: 139.

Incarnate: Louis MacNeice, *The Poetry of W.B. Yeats* (London: Faber and Faber, 1967 1941]): 15. Compare Merleau-Ponty again, from *The Phenomenology of Perception* (London: Routledge, 2012), p. lxxxiv: 'the only Logos that pre-exists is the world itself.'

Red grouse: Horatio Clare, *Running for the Hills: A Family Story* (London: John Murray, 2006): 108. (With thanks to Suzanna Saumarez.)

p.82

Freya Stark: 'Himyar, the Lizard', pp. 23–29 *Zodiac*: 27.

D.H. Lawrence: *The Complete Poems of D.H. Lawrence*, ed. David Ellis (Ware: Wordsworth Poetry Library, 2002): 282-84.

Nightingale: a composite of Richard Mabey, *The Barley Bird. Notes on the Suffolk Nightingale* (Woodbridge: Full Circle Editions, 2010): 17–18 and *The Book of Nightingales* (London: Sinclair-Stevenson, 1997): 8–9.

p.84

A pond with three swans: J.P. Donleavy, *J.P. Donleavy's Ireland. In All Her Sins And in Some of Her Graces* (London: Michael Joseph, 1986): 23–24.

Broadway: Henry Miller, *Sexus* (The Rosy Crucifixion, Book I), New York: Grove Weidenfeld, 1965, pp. 244–47. (With thanks to Clay Ramsay.)

Faërie: Robert Bringhurst, 'Introduction', pp. 11–18 in Alice Kane, *The Dreamer Awakes*, ed. Sean Kane (Peterborough: Broadview Press, 1995): 15, 16.

p.86

Geophany: Tim Robinson, 'Listening to the Landscape', *Irish Review* 14 (1993) 21-32: p. 32; reprinted in *Setting Foot on the Shores of Connemara and Other Writings* (Dublin: Lilliput, 1996) pp. 151–64.

Transfiguration: Gustav Theodor Fechner, quoted in William James, *A Pluralistic Universe* (Cambridge MA: Harvard University Press, 1977 [1909]): 76–77.

p.87

Primitive unity: Max Weber: 282.

Elements: Richard Jefferies, *The Story of my Heart* (London: Longman's Green & Co., 1883): 18, 98–99.

p.88

Shout of delight: J.B. Priestley, *Delight* (London: William Heineman Ltd., 1949): 224–225.

Enchantment swept: Cynthia Ozick, *Metaphor and Memory: Essays* (New York: Vintage Books, 1991): 140–41.

You're far away: Hoban, *The Moment Under the Moment*: 177.

Dusk: Karen Blixen, *Shadows on the Grass* (Harmondsworth: Penguin, 1984 [1960]): 97.

p.90

Our children learn: Ludwig Wittgenstein, *Culture and Value*, rev. edn, transl. Peter Winch and ed. G.H. von Wright (Oxford: Basil Blackwell, 1998): 81e (his emphasis).

With our bodies: D.H. Lawrence, *'Apropos of Lady Chatterley's Love' and Other Essays* (Harmondsworth: Penguin Books, 1961): 45.

When the Sun rises: William Blake, *Complete Writings*, ed. Geoffrey Keynes et al. (London: Oxford University Press, 1972: 555–56.

p.91

The tree: William Blake, *The Letters of William Blake* (1906), letter to the Reverend John Trusler (23 August 1799).

p.92

The world is wholly: Merleau-Ponty, *Phenomenology of Perception* (London: Routledge & Kegan Paul, 1962): 407.

p.93

Clear, bright: Charles Dickens, *A Christmas Carol*, final chapter.

Fichte: quoted in *Gunnar Beck, Fichte and Kant on Freedom, Rights, and Law* (Lanham: Lexington Books, 2008): 168.

p.94

Robin: R.S. Thomas, 'Song', in *Collected Poems* (London: Phoenix, 1993): 215.

Carolling: see Laurie Lee, *Village Christmas and Other Notes on the English Year* (London: Penguin Books, 2015): 7–10.

Snow Day: Stuart Jeffries, in *The Guardian* (3.2.09).

p.95

Blossom: Dennis Potter, interviewed by Melvyn Bragg, *Guardian* pamphlet (1994): 10.

9. Disenchantment

p.97

Licentious: Thomas Mann, *Death in Venice and Other Stories*, ed. David Luke (London: Vintage, 1988): 219.

Michael Hart's story: W.B. Yeats, *Irish Fairy Tales* (London: T. Fisher Unwin, n.d.): 51–52.

King of Elfland: Alice Kane, *Dreamer*: 145.

John Crowley: *Little, Big*: 90.

p.98

Cruelty: Montaigne, *Essays*: Bk. 2, Ch. 11.

S.S.: Jean Améry, *At the Mind's Limits. Contemplations by a Survivor on Auschwitz and its Realities*, transl. Sidney Rosenfeld and Stella P. Rosenfeld (London: Granta Books, 1999): 35–36.

Perfect fear: said to Harold Nicolson, quoted in Michael Sheldon, *Friends of Promise: Cyril Connolly and the World of Horizon* (London: Minerva, 1989): 64.

Why: Primo Levi, *If This is a Man and The Truce* (London: Sphere Books, 1987).

p.99

Auschwitz-Birkenau: Paul Feyerabend, *Farewell to Reason* (London: Verso, 1987): 313.

System: Max Horkheimer and T.W. Adorno, *The Dialectic of Enlightenment*, transl. Edmund Jephcott, ed. Gunzelin Schmid Noerr (Stanford: Stanford University Press, 2002 [1947]): 4.

Violence of unity: T.W. Adorno,

Persuasion: Ludwig Wittgenstein, *On Certainty*, ed. G.E.M. Anscombe and G.H. von Wright (Oxford: Blackwell, 1975): 81e.

Dissimilar things: Horkheimer and Adorno: 4.

p.100

Extirpation of animism: Horkheimer and Adorno: 2.

Reason and religion: Horkheimer and Adorno, 13. (I have used in preference here the earlier translation of John Cumming (New York: Continuum, 1994): 18.)

Cri de coeur: Nietzsche, in '"Reason" in Philosophy', *Twilight of the Idols*, section 2.

p.101

Scientistic writers: Richard Dawkins and Steven Weinberg respectively. See the following reference.

Mary Midgley: *Science and Poetry* (London: Routledge, 2001): 33. Midgley's discussion of these issues in this book and her *Science as Salvation: A Modern Myth and its Meaning* (London: Routledge, 1992) is superb. But see also the classic texts by Paul Feyerabend such as *Science in a Free Society* (London: NLB, 1978) and *Farewell to Reason* (London: Verso, 1987), and more recently John Dupré, *Human Nature and the Limits of Science* (Oxford: Clarendon Press, 2001).

Faith's irrationality: Horkheimer and Adorno: 15.

Megamachine: Lewis Mumford, *The Myth of the Machine*, 2 vols. (1967 and 1970).

Sad little song: Robert Bly, *A Little Book on the Human Shadow* (Rockport: Element, 1988): 71.

p.102

Auden: *Prose*, Vol. 3: 566.

p.103

We know: Eric Schmidt: quoted in the *TLS* (17.11.2017): 4.

Faust: for a wonderful fictional meditation on Faust in a novel for young adults of (as they say) all ages, see S.M. Saumarez, *The Akashic Record* (Knibworth Beauchamp:

Matador, 2014).

Sirens: Steven Shankman and Stephen Durrant, *The Siren and the Sage: Knowledge and Wisdom in Ancient Greece and China* (London: Cassell, 2000): 13.

Auden: *Prose*, Vol. 4: 133–34.

p.105

Effects of information and connectedness: see references above, plus James Williams, *Stand Out of the Light: Freedom and resistance in the attention economy* (Cambridge: Cambridge University Press, 2018) and Dave Eggers, 'The violations start with us.' An edited extract from the 2018 PEN H.G. Wells lecture on digital human rights, in a Human Rights Special Feature, *TLS* (21 and 28.12.2018).

Cultural fit: Ellen Ullman, quoted in the *TLS* (17.11.2017): 5.

Silicon Valley/internet/social media: see e.g. Ed Finn, *What Algorithms We Want* (Cambridge MA: MIT Press, 2017). Mark Bartholomew, *Adcreep* (Stanford: Stanford University Press, 2017), Jonathan Taplin, *Move Fast and Break Things* (Basingstoke: Macmillan, 2017), Ellen Ullman, *Life in Code* (St Louis: MCD, 2017), Rebecca Solnit, 'Easy Chair: Driven to Distraction', *Harper's Magazine* (May 2018): 7–9), Jaron Lanier, *Ten Arguments for Deleting Your Social Media Accounts Right Now* (London: The Bodley Head, 2018) and Carl Miller, *The Death of the Gods: The new global power grab* (London: William Heinemann, 2018).

p.106

'Weapons of math destruction': Cathy O'Neil, quoted in the *TLS* (24 and 31.8.2018): 21.

p.107

2016 survey of doctors: cited in *The New Yorker* (12. 11. 2018): 62.

p.108

Dimly lit: Bruno Schulz, *Collected Stories*, transl. Madeline G. Levine (Evanston: Northwestern University Press, 2018): 47.

Escape: Tolkien, OFS: 56.

10. Technoscience

p.109

On technoscience: for a fuller treatment, see my *Defending the Humanities: Metaphor, Nature and Science* (Rounded Globe, 2017):
https://roundedglobe.com/books/bccc6b49-3565-476b-9768-727d372044f8/ Defending%20the%20Humanities:%20Metaphor,%20Nature%20and%20Science/

Progress without hope: Chesterton, quoted in Paul Kingsnorth's *Real England: The Battle Against the Bland* (London: Portobello Books, 2008): 19.

p.110

Fathers of modern science: for a good overview, see John Henry, *The Scientific Revolution and the Origins of Modern Science* (London: Palgrave, 2001).

There exists nothing: René Descartes, *Oevres* Z19774 (Paris 1824–1826): 498–99. (Thanks to Garry Phillipson.)

p.111

Scientia universalis: Francis Bacon, *Meditationes Sacrae* (1597), in James Spedding, Robert Ellis and Douglas Heath (eds), *The Works of Francis Bacon (1887–1901)*, Vol. 7, p. 253; aphorism 28, *Novum Organum*, Book I (1620).

'If a thing can be done': *The Letters of J.R.R. Tolkien*, ed. Humphrey Carpenter and

Christopher Tolkien (London: HarperCollins, 2006): 246.

p.113

Parmenides: see Adriana Cavarero, *In Spite of Plato. A feminist rewriting of ancient philosophy*, transl. Serena Anderlini-D'Onofrio and Áine O'Healy (Cambridge: Polity Press, 1996).

p.114

Logical truths (Aristotle): for a good discussion of this as well as of phenomenology (as per Nietzsche's observation above), see Henri Bortoft, *Taking Appearance Seriously. The Dynamic Way of Seeing in Goethe and European Thought* (Edinburgh: Floris Books, 2012). (With thanks to Christopher J. Moore.)

p.115

All males: Auden, *Prose*, Vol. 6: 642.

p.116

Power is unlimited: Auden, *Prose*, Vol. 3: 322.

Hope without guarantees: Tolkien, *Letters*: 237 (no. 181).

p.117

Platonic misogyny: see Cavarero, *Plato*, and Plumwood, *Feminism*; also her 'Prospecting for Ecological Gold Among the Platonic Forms: A Response to Timothy Mahoney', *Ethics and the Environment* 2:2 (1997) 149–168.

Second Industrial Revolution: Yuval Noah Harari, accessed 15.4.15:

http://edge.org/conversation/yuval_noah_harari-daniel_kahneman-death-is-optional

11. Enchantment as a Way of Life

p.119

Tolkien: OFS: 18.

p.120

Wittgenstein: from his war diary, MS. 103, p. 30 (With thanks to Alfred Schmidt.)

p.121

Delicious melancholy: Julian Green, *Paris*, transl. J.A. Underwood (London: Penguin Books, 2012): 17.

Sweet melancholy: Jan Morris, *Trieste and the Meaning of Nowhere* (London: Faber and Faber, 2001): 4.

Blessed: Tolkien, *The Lord of the Rings*, Vol. 3: *The Return of the King* (London: George Allen & Unwin, 1955): Bk 3, ch. 9.

Iron cage: Weber, *The Protestant Ethic and the Spirit of Capitalism*, transl. Talcott Parsons (London: Routledge, 2001): 182.

Chesterton: *On Tremendous Trifles* (London: Hesperus Press, 2009): 6.

p.122

Vulnerable: Etel Adnan, from a notice beside one of her paintings in an exhibition in Basle in 2017.

p.124

The domestic: Zwicky, *Lyric*.

p.125

Imagination: this conception of the imagination as perception is virtually identical with Coleridge's 'Primary Imagination', although it was suggested to me rather by Merleau-Ponty.

Your eyes: Mark Twain, *The Wit and Wisdom of Mark Twain*, ed. Bob Blaisdell (Mineola:

Dover Publications, 2013): 66.

Unreachable: Judy Kravis, *Inside Barbara Kitten* (Garravagh: Boreen Books, 2014), n.p.

Canadian Mid-West: for high art by someone who has been able to access its enchantment, see poems by Jan Zwicky, e.g. 'Driving Northwest' and 'Prairie', pp. 30–31
in *Chamber Music: The Poetry of Jan Zwicky* (Waterloo: Wilfred Laurier University
Press, 2015).

p.126

Reality is an activity: this is the title of the poem.

Things-as-it-is: Suzuki, e.g. in a lecture 'Using Various Stones', given 8.9.1967, accessed
4.7.2018: http://cuke.com/pdf-2013/srl/v29-1-using-various-stones.pdf

A Bibliographical Note

I would like to mention some of the scholarly work upon which I have drawn. Chief among this is that of J.R.R. Tolkien, Max Weber, W.H. Auden, and still the best philosophical treatment of enchantment, R.W. Hepburn's *'Wonder' and Other Essays* (Edinburgh: Edinburgh University Press, 1984), as well as Jan Zwicky on the lyric. I should also mention G.K. Chesterton in this connection.

Second, there is work not directly on enchantment but which I have found vital for its understanding. It includes Maurice Merleau-Ponty's embodied phenomenology and David Abram's development of it as ecophenomenology, Henri Bortoft's elucidation of phenomenology *simpliciter* and related issues, inspired by Goethe; Gregory Bateson's ecological mind (including his rejection of both supernaturalism and mechanistic materialism, which echoes Weber's concrete magic) and its further development by Wendy Wheeler as biosemiotics; Paul Ricoeur's seminal work on metaphor, followed in importance by that of Philip Wheelwright; Ludwig Wittgenstein's later philosophy (not least its anti-Platonism); William James's radical pluralism and pragmatism; Montaigne's scepticism and humane humanism, Michel Serres's sensuous humanism, and John Ruskin's and Michael Oakeshott's conservative humanism; Val Plumwood's ecofeminism and Adriana Cavarero's feminist philosophy together with Liam Hudson and Bernadine Jacot's *The Way Men Think* (New Haven: Yale University Press, 1991); the psychoanalytic reflections of D.W. Winnicott; Sean Kane's ecocentric mythography; Paul Friedrich's scholarly paean to Aphrodite; the philosophical sinology of François Jullien; Eduardo Viveiros de Castro's perspectivism, as well as

Nietzsche's antecedent kind; Graham Harvey's animism; Martin Buber's animistic theology; Russell Hoban's essays as well as fiction; Karen Blixen's short stories and autobiographical reflections; Cyril Connolly's literary criticism as well as his unclassifiable *Unquiet Grave*; of poets, especially essays by Wallace Stevens, W.H. Auden, Seamus Heaney, and C.K. Williams; and the musical philosophies of Vladimir Jankélévitch and Victor Zuckerkandl. I have also benefitted greatly from reading Proust, as well as three excellent secondary sources: George Stambolian, *Marcel Proust and the Creative Encounter* (Chicago: University of Chicago Press, 1972); Jean-François Revel, *On Proust*, trans. Martin Turnell (London: Hamish Hamilton, 1972); and Roger Shattuck, *Proust's Binoculars: A Study of Memory, Time, and Recognition in* A la recherche du temps perdu (London: Chatto & Windus, 1964).

I have read a considerable amount of more narrowly academic work on enchantment (or what is described as enchantment) and often found it to be unhelpful. Many authors seem to feel they can ignore enchantment's distinctiveness and conflate it, without cost, with the fantastic, the surreal, the Gothic, the uncanny, the sublime of Kant and/or Burke, or simply the Romantic. Changing the nature of what you are studying to suit your critical tools, rather than the other way round, does not count as enlightened. Nor does appropriating a concept that you haven't bothered to try to understand simply in order to be able to use it in your favourite theoretical schema. And in that respect, anyone who still runs together enchantment and magic has hardly got started. Finally, the vulgar Platonic belief that style is separable from something called 'content', and therefore unimportant, is also never a good sign. (I have discussed a few of these issues in my 'Enchantment and Modernity', referenced above under Chapter 2.)

However, I have the impression that this situation is changing for the better. One promising sign is Peik Ingman, Terhi Utriainen, Tuija Hovi and Måns Broo (eds), *The Relational Dynamics of Enchantment and Sacrilization* (Sheffield: Equinox Publishing, 2016). (I have reviewed this collection for the journal *Material Religion*, 2018.) Others are Genevieve Lloyd, *Reclaiming Wonder*.

After the Sublime (Edinburgh: Edinburgh University Press, 2018) and Sophia Vasalou, *Wonder: A Grammar* (Albany: SUNY Press, 2015), both excellent, although they came to my attention after this book was essentially complete. I also enjoyed Mathew Del Nevo's *The Work of Enchantment* (London: Routledge, 2011), although I don't agree with restricting that work to art. Finally, the literary criticism of Rita Felski, advocating the recovery of a sense of wonder, is encouraging.

Acknowledgements

I have received a great deal of help with this book, seen and unseen, and I am deeply grateful to the following people. Let me add that very few of them, if any, would agree with everything I've said. In fact, there is something for almost everyone to disagree with in this book. That may be one of the good things about it, or a sign of something good. In the case of my close readers, however, it makes their support all the more sterling.

Susan Peters, in pride of place, has given me unflagging support throughout, and she and Michael J. Winship, Christopher J. Moore, Clay Ramsay and Leslie Van Gelder have kindly read and helpfully commented on the whole manuscript more than once. I am also extremely grateful to Christopher J. Moore for taking me on, plus his invaluable editorial advice, support and guidance. Neil Platts, Wendy Wheeler, Liz Greene and Anthony Thorley have read most chapters and made many perceptive suggestions. Adam Dickerson also read it in draft and commented helpfully. David Abram has been a positive influence, both in print and in conversation. In the course of earlier drafts of this book, Sean Kane and I exchanged chapters from his excellent forthcoming work on wonder to my benefit. And I owe Graham Harvey a particular debt for having accepted my proposed paper on 'Magic vs Enchantment' for a conference at Winchester College in 1997, which was the start of my consciously considering this subject.

I am also grateful to Kigen-san Licha, Elena Bernardini, Garry Phillipson, Nigel Cooper, Ruth Thomas-Pellicer, Eduardo Viveiros de Castro, Katherine Coles, Garry Todd, Mark Dickinson, Amy Whitehead, Scott Black, Geoffrey Cornelius, Martine Sandor, Victor Postnikov, Suzanna Saumarez, Fabrizio Manco, Andy

Barritt, Alf and Natasha Seegert, Laurence Coupe and Stephen Fitzpatrick for helpful exchanges and insights; as well as to Val Plumwood, whose death ended our conversation much too soon.

I also appreciate having had the moral support of Tim and Mairead Robinson, Robert MacFarlane, Chrissy Philp, Ray Keenoy, Rebecca Burrill, Alexandra Kreuzeder, Alfred Schmidt, Jesper Siberg, Jo Dubiel, Lykke Strunk, Sargon Donabed, Daniela Vogt, Jan Zwicky, Lou Marinoff, Tim Winship, Woody Wood, Bernadette Brady, Darby Costello and Stephen Frank, Robert Chandler, Graeme Tobyn, James Longworth, Mahesh Patel, Deborah Bird Rose, Paul Reade, Graham Douglas, Sheryl Cotleur, Chris Beckett, Darrelyn Gunzburg, Sabrina Briggs, Stone Fitzgerald, Annabel Chaos, Beate Süss, Walter Weiss, Lisa Mendes, Steele, Mark and Kathy Curry, Clare Hedin, John Swain, Charles Stephens, Guglielmo Spirito, Brian and Melanie Gold, Sharon Blackie, Jana Nekulová, Joshua Ramey, Kate Tomas, Iain McGilchrist, Sylva Faye, Nancy Eaton, Ian Whyte, Petra Stapp, Joe Gray, Ralfee Finn, Brian Kennedy, Richard Pinchen, Peter Moore, Diane Hirst, Paul Anderson, Mary Bisbee-Beek, Garey Mills, Heinrich Reventlow, Sonia Fargue, Kirk Little, Peter Case, Xavier Curry, Angela Voss, Patrick Joyce, Marlene Roeder, James Frazier, James Brockbank, Elnur Nuraliyev, Bernard Eccles, Ronald Hutton, Naomi Horoiwa, Simon Saumarez, Michael York, Chantal Allison, Celia Gunn, Laëtitia Laguzet, Franco Manni, Audrey Morrell, Nicholas Campion and the late Ursula Le Guin. (I would probably have been able to include Russell Hoban if I hadn't left it too late.) I would also like to thank Isao Miura for permission to use his painting for the cover, and Farzad Abaeian and Anne Pennington for their technical help.

Thanks also to Polly's Tea Room in Hampstead and The Literary Café in Tufnell Park: independent cafés of a vanishing kind (with character) but thankfully still here. The same is true of Hunter's Hotel in County Wicklow and the Pensione Bencistà in Fiesole, where I sometimes took refuge to write. Cyril Connolly's description of the writer's 'rightful place of composition' as 'the small single unluxurious "retreat" of the twentieth century, the hotel bedroom' remains true.

Finally, I gratefully acknowledge the inspiration and guidance of all those thinkers, writers and teachers, living as well as no longer present in the flesh, upon whose work I have also drawn. The well is deep, the water fresh and clear.

Index

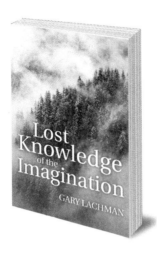

Floris Books

For news on all our **latest books,**
and to receive **exclusive discounts,**
join our mailing list at:

florisbooks.co.uk

Plus subscribers get a FREE book
with every online order!

We will never pass your details to anyone else.